Without Principal Goolsby's sacrifice, perseverance, and willingness to learn on the fly, ISK could have never experienced the recognition we received from the American and Afghan governments, the White House, families, and students. Kudos to Gail for finally getting the story and record out.

– Dr. Byron Greene, ISK Director 2005-2009

Gail's exemplary leadership paved the path for many children and their families to dream for a better tomorrow especially when the reality all around them screamed hopelessness! Gail's life journey and her experiences in Kabul and ISK are worth chronicling. Our world desperately needs more women like Gail to share their stories.

– Dilip Joseph, Humanitarian, Author of Kidnapped by the Taliban

I am Ahmad Sayer Daudzai, graduate of the International School of Kabul (ISK). I have served as a diplomat for four years when I was appointed as the Vice Consul of Afghanistan in Istanbul, Turkey. The legacy of [Mrs. Goolsby's] efforts lives on in each of us ISK graduates as we embark upon the journey of rebuilding our country.

[When ISK closed], I realized how important ISK and Mrs. Goolsby's leadership was for Afghanistan. I owe much of what I achieved to my parents, Mrs. Goolsby, and the entire ISK team.

– Ahmad Sayer Daudzai, Co-Founder of Capital Star Insurance, Founder of Velocity Solar, CEO of Velocity Consulting

ISK gave me the opportunity to keep my children in their homeland and continue to serve my country for more than a decade. The high educational standard of ISK is testament to the management skills of Gail Goolsby. She played a key role in the success of my daughters who went on to acquiring higher education from some of the best universities around the world. Gail Goolsby's commitment...made the ISK project a success.

– *Mohammad Umer Daudzai, Former Interior Minister of the Islamic Republic of Afghanistan, Chief of Political Office of the Protection and Stability Council of Afghanistan*

I am a member of Afghanistan's Parliament, representing the Kochi people of Afghanistan. Over the years, I watched how [Mrs. Goolsby] led the teachers and students in a confident, strong, just, and inspiring manner. I was comforted by...a school that could intellectually stimulate and develop my daughters.

– *Elay Ershad, Afghanistan Member of Parliament (MP)*

Along with many others, I am of the opinion that ISK represented "the best hope for Afghanistan." Mrs. Gail Goolsby provided leadership to a team of teachers who accepted and loved students from varied backgrounds and patiently taught them a "new way" to think, act, and reason through sharing knowledge and sharing life. Mrs. Goolsby modeled female leadership in such a way that she was loved and respected by those she served.

– *Dr. Joe Hale, President, Oasis International Schools, Inc.*

UNVEILED TRUTH

UNVEILED TRUTH

Lessons I Learned
Leading the International
School of Kabul

GAIL GOOLSBY

Unveiled Truth: Lessons I Learned Leading the International School of Kabul

Published by Live Well Press

Printed in the United States of America

Kabul Photograph by Khalid Ahmadzai

Stock Photo by Ifrah Akhter on Unsplash

Author Photo by Michael Bankston

Editing and Book Interior by Melissa Jagears

To protect the privacy of individuals who are still living, some names and details have been changed. The following is the author's personal recollection of the events.

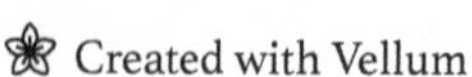

Created with Vellum

To my dad,
You taught me many life lessons and somehow made me believe you delighted in me no matter what mistakes I made. I was the proverbial apple off your tree and that was just fine with me.

To ISK students, families and staff,
You took a chance on a new school with a rookie principal and demonstrated fully what courage and perseverance can accomplish. You are still doing so all over the world. You made my Kabul lessons worthwhile and you are forever imprinted in my memory.

CONTENTS

Author's Note xi

1. When Still Waters Start to Rock and Roll 1
2. Prepare for the Worst 14
3. The Pain of Obedience 23
4. The Precious Pearl of Education 33
5. Lift Up Your Eyes 46
6. The Clash and Crash of Cultures 53
7. Only the Strong Survive 64
8. For the Good of Girls 75
9. Whom Shall I Fear? 89
10. Surviving Deep Waters 101
11. Safety is Overrated 114
12. Don't Judge a Book (or a Librarian) by its Cover 127
13. No Place to Hide 141
14. The Power to Change Comes from Within 152
15. Try Something New 162
16. The Fine Art of Failure 173
17. Who's in Charge? 185
18. Making the Best of a Bad Situation 198
19. There's No Place like Home to Heal 211
20. Not Finished Yet 223
21. Learning and Living Well 235

Acknowledgments 257
About the Author 263

Author's Note

I never wanted to live anywhere besides the U.S.A. How I ended up in Kabul, Afghanistan for seven years still surprises me.

When I signed a two-year contract with Oasis International Schools out of Southaven, MS to become the K-12 Principal/Counselor of the International School of Kabul (ISK), no one had said it would be easy.

Three of the many "strikes" against me included: being a woman, being an American, and heading up an international co-ed school where Taliban extremism still pulsed through the culture in 2005. It was an amazing time and I don't want to forget it, even the tough times, because there will never be another experience like it for me.

The following chapters cover many of my memories and favorite stories, but some names and details are changed or combined with additional events to protect the personal lives of people I came to respect and who need such consideration for their safety.

It wasn't only hard for Americans to live in Afghanistan; it was hard (and still is) for other foreigners and even Afghans to navigate war and changing times in that desperate place.

The culture and the history of Afghanistan reveal a

resilient people that should inspire respect. I have no political agenda to promote. I don't pretend to know the perfect military solution or how international communities should support the failing country.

From my experience, I recognize the power of individuals dedicated to helping others, especially under the umbrella of Christian service, and through education to change a culture and a country. I know absolutely that what we did at ISK was important and far-reaching in its impact on Afghanistan and the world. And in the process of working for change in that faraway place, I was also changed.

The lessons I wrote about in this book and learned during my seven years can be applied to anyone, anytime, anywhere. Life challenges may rise out of unique circumstances, but resulting truth learned by dealing with people, change, disappointment, failure, and perseverance can be applied broadly. Perhaps you will resonate with some of the life lessons in the following pages. I hope you will find encouragement to continue growing and learning to live well, even when life is difficult.

I

When Still Waters Start to Rock and Roll

I'd been waiting three years for this dream getaway to celebrate twenty-five years of marriage to my husband, Michael. The Caribbean sunshine sparkled on the clear blue waters surrounding our cruise ship. The gourmet food, on-board service, evening entertainment, and island excursions promised a restful, exotic experience. What could be more perfect?

On our first cruise morning, Michael sat beside me in the matching lounge chair on our private balcony, freshly-showered, the silver streaks above his temples glimmering in the sunlight. He reached out and took my hand. "I know I resisted this trip, but I'm really glad you persevered. What are you thinking?"

I leaned back farther in my chair and smiled at the seagulls riding the warm air currents. "How we deserve this vacation and I'm not really missing kids or home or work. You?"

"Well." He looked up at those birds, then slowly turned toward me. "I would like us to talk about our next twenty-five years and what that would look like."

Our eyes met briefly, then I turned back to the peaceful view and released his hand.

Uh-oh. I knew his past couple of years in business after leaving a full-time pastor position were not necessarily fulfilling him. But for me, my time as the school counselor at our local K-12 Christian school was humming along just fine. Life seemed easier than ever with only one of our three children still at home and entering her senior year of high school. I wasn't looking for major changes beyond the upcoming empty-nest stage which sounded pretty good then.

I couldn't turn to look at him, afraid of what was going to come out of his mouth next.

Michael stretched out his legs and folded his hands over his still trim torso. His trademark deep sigh joined the conversation. "I feel a need to go back into full-time ministry somewhere."

"Okay..." I slowly sat up straight in my chair to face him, sadly shutting out the hypnotic relaxation of the shining ocean. "What do you have in mind?"

The perfect part of our trip seemed to dangle dangerously in the air. I willed myself not to jump into interrogation/frustration mode just yet. My dear husband has an invisible bucket list long enough for four people. If we had followed through with every degree program he had ever expressed interest in, well, we would be broke, and the string of letters behind his name would be embarrassing.

I'd learned early on not to pull sticks from my nest whenever Michael began to describe a new career or skill he wanted to pursue. Not that I didn't get nervous and vocalize my incredulity at some of his ideas. I mean, there may be people who can be pastors *and* doctors *and* lawyers *and* farmers *and* politicians *and* successful businessmen *and* yes, even cowboys all in one lifetime, but what normal person could?

"Well, I feel a pull to move overseas." He searched my face, always known to give a telling expression.

Hmm, here we go again. I couldn't think of a positive response and didn't want to totally ruin our vacation, so I sat in silence.

We are the quintessential opposites-attract-but-can-hardly-live-together type couple. *Feel* is the absolute correct term for his default processing verb; mine being *think.* I did not feel this same pull at all. We had both traveled overseas for a number of humanitarian aid trips, together and separately in the past decade, but move overseas? I definitely did not feel or think we should do anything of the sort.

"Like where, exactly?" I finally asked. My heart rate increased as I waited for the answer.

"How would you feel about going to Afghanistan?"

Great. As stunned as I was to actually hear him say the destination, I was not completely surprised. I returned my gaze to the beauty of the Caribbean and let my own heavy sigh escape unchecked.

After 9/11, Michael had intentionally studied Islamic culture for deeper understanding and had shared what he learned with interested learners in our local church through sermons and classes on Sundays.

He'd gotten involved with non-governmental organizations (NGOs) to deliver food, medicine, prosthetics, eyeglasses, and wheelchairs to villages around Kabul. His first Afghanistan trip took place in the fall of 2002. Throughout the country, he'd seen Afghans living in poverty with sickness, disabilities, and other afflictions rarely seen in modern cultures. The devastation impacted his tender pastor's heart. He had a second trip scheduled a couple of months after our cruise.

I supported his desire to help, but my response to the stories and photos from his trip was: *That is no place to live, not for a woman, and certainly not for me.*

I felt no differently now, so I remained silent.

"Would you be willing to at least pray with me about this? Starting this week on our trip?" He took my hand and squeezed it with a pleading expression.

How could I refuse to pray? But I had a lot of thinking to do and needed some time to envision how this could possibly work. "Okay, how about we give it four to six months of prayer, separately and together but without telling others? *If* God is leading this idea, He will be the One to speak to us and no one else. Agreed?"

Michael smiled. I didn't.

Then he added what I thought would prove to be my escape clause. "Hon, if this is meant to be, there will be a call for you, too, not just for me."

Right. I felt certain that I would not be answering *that* call.

From my perspective, all aspects of our life seemed satisfactory already, perhaps even noteworthy. I historically bloomed wherever I was planted, finding plenty of organizations and activities in which to offer my energy and leadership skills. My career path included some impressive accomplishments, such as pioneering women's groups during our years in seminary and establishing the counseling program at St. Joseph Christian School (SJCS) in my hometown. I completed my first graduate degree while working full-time and parenting three active teenagers. The lines connecting my life made sense, with few out-of-the-blue sharp turns. Personality assessments would not profile me as a high-risk taker.

Afghanistan was definitely under the high-risk category. I wasn't honestly committing to praying for a *yes*, but more to discern that *no* would be the right answer.

Two weeks after our anniversary trip, I was working in my counseling office. Students weren't in the building yet; only staff was present, gearing up for the new school year. My boss popped into my office to relate the highlights of a recent Christian leadership conference he attended for school administrators. In the midst of his reporting, he innocently asked, "So did you know there is an American K-12 private school starting up in Kabul next month?"

My boss attended our church and knew Michael had visited Afghanistan but had no knowledge of our cruise discussions.

A school? I kept my eyes on the master schedule spreadsheet before me and willed my face to remain expressionless. I wished he had stopped talking earlier.

Picture a heavy, loosely woven fishing net with weights on the corners slowly dropping from my ceiling.

I felt like I was in danger of being ensnared rather than called. If anything could attract me to the Afghanistan possibility, it would be a school. *Really, God? You cannot be serious.*

I did not share the Afghan school news with Michael that night. No doubt he would think it was God giving me options. I was not so sure. The next day, in the secrecy of my counselor office, I caved into curiosity and conducted what I thought would be an anonymous, online investigation of this new Kabul school.

There *was* a school opening in Afghanistan like my boss had said. The need was real. Families were heading to newly freed Afghanistan to help rebuild the government and bring relief to the massive suffering from war, poverty, sickness, drought, and Taliban oppression. The expats and repatriating Afghans needed quality education for their children. School staff would have to raise their own salaries and start from scratch with makeshift facilities and donated supplies and books.

Really? After years of making only pennies in the private Christian school sector, now I should work for nothing? On top of that, ask people to contribute to pay my expenses? No, no, no. Surely God would not ask me to do this. It made absolutely no sense.

On the day following my internet discovery, the phone rang in my counseling office.

"Is this Gail Goolsby?" the caller asked. "I'm Joe Hale, the President of Oasis International Schools calling from the U.S. home office in Southaven, Mississippi."

Gulp. "Yes, this is Gail," I managed to squeak out.

"We were just in a staff prayer meeting asking God who He would send to help us with this incredible opportunity in Kabul. I saw you inquired on our website and wanted to personally call you."

He made the timing of my query sound so heavenly orchestrated that before I knew it, I had agreed to apply to join the Kabul educational team sometime in the future. I hung up the phone that now seemed to be blazing hot and part of the conspiracy to trap me into this crazy scheme. *How was this was happening? To me?*

The imaginary net lowered. Now I had to tell Michael. As I expected, his eyes lit up with excitement and possibility. He wisely said little as he viewed my somber face and tightly crossed arms.

"Let's continue to pray, dear." He held me and I felt a little less alone. But I was scared this might be the right thing for us.

Joe had mentioned the couple starting the new school would be in the city during Michael's upcoming trip to Kabul in September of 2003. He hoped they could connect.

I doubted that would happen. How would they find each other in such a big city?

"Guess who I am having dinner with tonight, dear?" Michael's email from Kabul greeted me one morning as I opened my computer at work. I could see him smiling from ear-to-ear in my mind.

Great. But I can still say no. I slammed the laptop closed.

By this time, the circle of folks who knew what we were considering had widened. The team members with Michael in Afghanistan were aware this trip carried more personal significance than only serving the needs there. A few selected friends and family were recruited to confidentially pray on our behalf about this future cross-cultural idea.

"How is Michael's trip going?" many people from church and school asked. I responded with a cheery affirmation to all except for a couple of very close girlfriends. They stayed empathically quiet as they heard my reports from Michael about the new school and his connection with the founders. They didn't want this to be my future any more than I did.

After his return, Michael and I had several serious conversations while lying in bed unable to sleep. He was dealing with jet lag. I was dealing with dread and disbelief. Both lent to short nights and long, fatigued days.

The opportunities for ministry and business he experienced on the recent trip and the addition of the school brought a plausible outline into focus. I couldn't deny the way things were shaping up for both of us. The sense of ensnarement increased, not painfully, but not comfortably. I still had many questions.

It was time to break out of our small group of confidants and gather all the wisdom we could about relocating overseas. We met with several leaders, wise in areas of ministry and family, and living a life of faith. Our church and a special group of lifetime friends formed a sending team committed to help us pray, plan, and prepare for our possible transition. Our two oldest children, Sarah and John, were cautious but encouraging.

The youngest, Anna, refused to even talk about it. She ran to her room in tears when we broached the subject. We probed enough to finally uncover her paralyzing thoughts.

"I need you to wait until I've finished at least one year of college. What if I can't cut it? I need you here, not there!" she cried.

Her tears tore at my mother's heart. Having worked in the same school where my three children attended for virtually every year of their lives, I was trying to picture being across the globe from them. I couldn't, but Michael seemed to be okay with the separation.

"They'll be fine. It will be okay," were his frequent responses to my worries about splitting up our family.

Michael began inquiring into faith-based agencies working in Kabul. With his combination of business background and ministry training, everyone wanted him. Of course, these were not salaried opportunities, so our team began to investigate fund-raising in order to handle our financial needs. With so much attention being given to the rebuilding of Afghanistan, the recruiters offered quick timelines, some as soon as my school year ended in June 2004.

Whoa, wait just a minute. That is way too soon!

I wanted Michael to slow down, but he can be wide-open to new things and blind to details impacting others. Thankfully, many on our team were also seeing the need for careful, methodical progress, rather than jumping in faith with eyes closed. I loved our team! They could speak the same things I had already voiced to Michael, but he listened to them with more patience and less defensiveness.

We postponed potential departure plans to the summer of 2005, to focus on Anna's transition to college, Sarah's December wedding, and fund-raising. My sheer panic subsided, but I still needed more information to be sure this was the right decision. For me.

So I traveled to Kabul for a week in September 2004 with my husband and a group from our church. Exhausted from the full days of travel just to get to Dubai, I met the bleakness of Kabul in the chaotic, small airport in disbelief and disdain. I observed no orderly lines through passport control or anywhere. There were precious few baggage carts, except ancient ones in the hands of persistent independent contractors. I smelled the effects of no air conditioning and too little body deodorant.

I felt as if I had left reasonable life far behind.

I heard no English and saw almost no women. Male travelers on our flight outnumbered females probably ten to one. With my body conservatively covered from head to toe in the penetrating heat, I wanted to be somewhere else, anywhere else.

This is no place to live, I thought as I gazed out the window of the shuttle van on the road from the airport to our guesthouse. Random horns blared, traffic moved according to drivers' whims and boldness, and dust blew. Everything looked dirty and broken down. Buildings were in shambles and riddled with bullet and rocket holes. People were everywhere, again mostly men, who wore serious, unfriendly expressions on their leathered faces.

This is the end of the earth.

"Aren't you excited to be here?" asked one of the women in our group on the seat beside me. Women were in the back of the van and men in the front as Afghan Muslim culture demanded.

I smiled weakly at her and turned my face back to the overwhelming scenes on the streets. Tears welled up. *Maybe with some rest and time to adjust, I will feel differently. Other people have come here and found fulfilling and significant Kingdom service. Maybe I will, too. Maybe.*

Each day at our guesthouse, I awoke at sunrise as the call to prayer blasted over the loudspeaker from the local mosque in the neighborhood.

"*Allahu Akbar. Allahu Akbar. Allahu Akbar. Allahu Akbar.*"

During the visits to community centers and hospital clinics, I met many interesting and dedicated international workers and male Afghan business and political leaders. They were working together on varied projects to improve health care, education, job training, and basic living for Afghans everywhere. I ate lots of nan (Afghan bread), chips (fried potatoes), and Kabuli Palau (a rice dish) and soon became acquainted with major stomach issues. This slimmer-faster plan, as I dubbed it, helped me lose seven pounds in one week. Not a good thing.

I wrote daily in my journal, trying to make sense of the conflicting thoughts flooding me. My head buzzed with a bizarre mixture of assessing real possibilities and I-don't-want-this-to-be-my-life kind of thinking. *Was I really going to end up here? Would I find anything to like? To actually enjoy?*

"How are you doing? How is your stomach?" My husband quickly squeezed my hand but released it since men and women, even those who were married or related, were not to have physical contact in public. Enjoying a rare private moment during that Kabul trip, we walked on a dusty street near the guesthouse. "Sorry we couldn't get a room together." (The people in charge of the guesthouse required men to be in one dorm room, women in the other.)

"The fifty-cent, local medicine really did the trick. I feel weak but the crisis is past." I adjusted my required headscarf to get relief from the heat. "The bigger jolt to my system is seeing all this in person." I glanced over at a small child sorting through the corner trash pile looking for something to sell while his mother, ensconced in a blue burka, stood nearby. "Even your photos couldn't give the full picture of how primitive and desperate everything is."

"There is much to do here, that's for sure." Michael smiled, nodded, and bowed in greeting to Afghan men we passed on the street, holding his hand to his chest, mirroring what they did to indicate honor and respect. I was looked at briefly, then ignored as if invisible, the typical cultural response to women. Maddening and insulting in my American mindset.

"But I see you are loving this. The poverty and unending needs don't seem to get to you. I notice you chatting at breakfast and throughout the day to the Afghan male workers and drivers at the guesthouse who speak English."

With just that slight intro, Michael enthusiastically recounted the details of each man, his family, and some of his Afghanistan life challenges. Clearly, my husband was enraptured with the potential of making a difference in this impoverished place. I was not and he didn't seem to notice my withdrawal from the conversation.

I felt very alone, even as we walked side-by-side.

However, the day we visited Kabul International Academy (KIA), then in its second year, everything changed for me.

"Here is our soccer field and PE space," explained the young male teacher giving us a tour of the large home and yard serving as the school. "We have almost fifty students now, and more families want to send their children every day. The Afghan schools are not able to offer much after so much war and no resources."

I saw several Afghan and a few international students joyfully attending KIA to learn from qualified, dedicated teachers. In the classrooms, I heard solid instruction and students responding eagerly. The looks on their faces were recognizable to me as a career educator: interest, enthusiasm, pride. These were the brightest images gathered so far in my Kabul experience.

I sensed my resistance to moving to Afghanistan dissipating. I could make a difference here, offer something rare and prized—a quality education.

"Please come join us here," requested one of the six twenty-something, heroic, hard-working teachers at the school dinner that night. "We would love for a married couple with wisdom (insert *age* here) to help us become a more balanced and effective team. We need experienced school leadership."

I cried silently in the van as we left KIA. A school without an administrator is like a brick wall without mortar. It is functional, but not stable. I felt like I was leaving behind sick children who needed a parent.

I didn't see anyone else lining up for this administrative role.

Things happened just like Michael predicted. For the first time, I sensed my own undeniable call to Afghanistan.

The net dropped to envelop me.

Would I come to be grateful for this next season of life, marriage, and career experience in such a dreary, reduced, even oppressed place? I am a realistic yet hopeful person, but this Kabul future was proving to be my biggest challenge yet to believe that our life was changing for the good. If not for my faith, if only looking at the circumstances, I would have refused to move forward. But I knew God loved me and would take care of me, somehow, someway, even in desolate Afghanistan.

A small piece of anticipation, maybe only simple curiosity, began to creep into my heart and make its way toward my head. For now, that little bit of positive emotion was enough for me to accept that I'd been caught.

The Unveiled Truth: I like to make my own plans, hopefully remembering to use prayer and God's wisdom.

But our personal life plans are often interrupted, even hijacked, by someone or something. When life goes awry, it's best we reserve doomsday judgment until we've gathered enough information to determine whether or not we're simply scared about change.

When opportunities call, don't refuse to pick up the phone and listen. Otherwise, you could be missing out on the grandest adventure of your life.

Is there a new, maybe even frightening, challenge you're ignoring because you're afraid of change?

2

Prepare for the Worst

I signed up to join the staff at the Kabul school though I had no idea what I'd be doing.

"I would like to visit you in January," Joe Hale, the president of Oasis International Schools, wrote in an email late fall 2004. "It would be great to meet your family and friends and get better acquainted."

I agreed to the visit, believing it was a kind and courteous gesture, for I knew how busy this man must be with nineteen schools under his charge. I was eager to talk over whether or not they'd need me for position of counselor or whether the school would be better served if I were to teach kindergarten. But within minutes of our first in-person conversation, I realized he'd come with his own agenda. He didn't just want me to be a part of the school, he wanted me to lead the school.

I put my tea down and leaned forward on the love seat in my Missouri living room. "Whoa, wait a minute! I have no experience as a lead administrator. After visiting Afghanistan, I cannot picture how that would even work. A woman, an American woman, in that male-dominated place leading the only co-ed school in the country? Thanks for the compliment, but no."

If living in that place would not be stressful enough, away from my kids and friends, he wants me to take on the bottom-line responsibility of a new school? Easy for him to ask, but I would be scared to death every day and have no idea what to do next.

"We have a stack of teachers applying for Kabul, but no one with as much administration experience as you. Talk to your coworkers at St. Joseph Christian and ask them what they think." Joe glanced over at Michael who nodded in affirmation.

I shot my husband a dark look and he stopped nodding.

During early morning staff devotions, I cleared my throat to speak and looked into the faces of dear friends. Many were not only coworkers but parents of children I had taught in kindergarten. Many instructed and impacted the academic, musical, athletic, and spiritual growth of my own three kids over the years. "As you know, Michael and I are making preparations to move to Afghanistan. A new school is forming in Kabul and I have been asked to consider leading the school."

A few soft gasps erupted, and eyes grew wide at this news. "Joe Hale, the President of Oasis International Schools, is in town and will be coming to SJCS today and tomorrow. He is interested in speaking with any of you who are comfortable sharing your thoughts about my leadership abilities. Please, feel free to speak honestly. I don't know that this is the right plan. I really hope it isn't, to be truthful. I need to hear God speak to gain confidence for such a step."

While the group earnestly prayed for me, I felt choked up

and tried not to cry. I loved this workplace and it held so many pieces of my heart and important stages of my career development. *How could I find such a supportive team with strangers in a strange land?*

Later that day, one couple I deeply respected, who had both worked at St. Joseph Christian for many years and had pastor fathers with overseas experience, came to see me. The wife taught fourth grade and the husband was a high school history teacher who had coached all my kids in volleyball or basketball.

"Gail, I believe this is a perfect fit for your leadership skills and heart for education," the wife said to me outside my counseling office. "I told Joe that even though you hadn't been a headmaster or principal before, that you could be effective in that role and they would be blessed to have you. We have total faith that you can do this with God's help." She gave me an affectionate hug and her less-chatty spouse smiled, patting my shoulder in confirmation of his wife's words.

Others came forward in the two days of Joe's visit with similar encouragement. Joe had also made appointments with our personal sending team members. I received notes and calls from them, relaying the same message, "You can do this. We believe in you, and God will help."

I entered into the solitude of my office on the last day of Joe's visit and gazed out at the playground where elementary children ran and squealed in delight with innocent freedom. The image of the brick wall with no mortar flooded back into my mind.

At dinner that night, I listened to Joe chat about our talented and dedicated sending team. Michael filled in details of his past church and business involvement with the various members. Joe reviewed his flight itinerary with Michael for the next morning's trip to the Kansas City airport.

I knew I had to give my answer to the leadership question. When serving one of my trademark homemade pies for dessert, I decided to get it over with.

"These last couple days have been rough," I began. "I wish I could join the Kabul school in a role with which I am more familiar, like kindergarten or counseling. But I know full well if there is a leadership void, we would all suffer, and I can't be responsible for that risk if I can do something about it." Both Joe and Michael waited with a forkful of cherry pie in hand and hopeful expressions.

"I seem to be the only person doubting my ability to take on a top leadership role. You, Joe, my school colleagues, and our sending team have all affirmed the idea. My two bosses at St. Joseph Christian made it clear that I have what it takes and already know plenty about administration from my counseling role and years in the classroom."

After a sip of water, I continued, "Okay, here is my decision. I will take the principal position. I can handle teachers, students, parents, scheduling, and curriculum. But you'll need to find a male director to deal with all the Afghan men in government and security. I seriously doubt they will respect me."

Raising his fist in a victory pump, Joe smiled broadly and glanced at Michael. I reluctantly looked at my husband, knowing full well his thoughts, but still needing to hear him say out loud, "Good for you, dear. You will be the best principal ever." He reached over and squeezed my hand with gratitude and admiration shining in his eyes.

"One more thing," Joe said as we drank our last cups of coffee and tea. "I don't know any couples living overseas who don't work in the same organization. Michael, I suggest you join Oasis and serve the school in some capacity, also."

Joe was a passionate salesman, and Michael reluctantly agreed to work at the school for one year. He'd been planning to enroll in language school and work among the local Afghans as he had in previous visits. His heart to help was big and he was grateful for the school giving me a reason to enter into our Afghanistan journey. If working at the school would be best for us as a couple, he was willing to give it at least a year and postpone his own agenda.

Over the next several months, we scurried to complete a myriad of tasks before departing for Kabul in early August. We trained replacements and prepared to leave our jobs. I visited the Oasis home office for international school administrator training. We updated our wills and obtained necessary immunizations and medical clearances, including authorization for our family doctor to make end-of-life decisions which freaked out our daughters.

"In Muslim cultures, they bury bodies within twenty-four hours," my husband explained to the strained faces of our three children and new son-in-law. "Our insurance will cover the repatriating of our remains back to the U.S., or we could just be buried in Afghanistan and you wouldn't have to worry about any of that."

Anna broke into tears and buried her head into her sister's shoulder. "If you think you are going to be killed there, why are you going?" she managed between sobs.

Sarah stroked Anna's hair and chose her words carefully while clasping tightly to her new husband's hand. "I know you have to cover all the possible problems and solutions. But, if something does happen, we don't want your bodies left over there!"

"You know." Our son John stopped petting our family dog and looked at his sisters. "It would save a bunch of money to do cremation over body burial and casket services."

"Shut up, John!" Anna threw a pillow at him which he easily caught.

"What? It would be. When you work at a funeral home, you learn this stuff." He looked for confirmation from Michael who also knew about funeral arrangements as a pastor.

"Doesn't matter how much it would cost. Mom and Dad are not going to die in Afghanistan!" Anna shot back at him.

I did not meet the gaze of any of my precious children. I had no words and hated every bit of this conversation.

Michael went over and knelt in front of the two girls and took their hands. "Listen. We don't expect anything to happen, but we need to be prepared. We've talked to Dr. Griffin about this, and he will help you if something happens to us medically. You know all of the people on our support team, and they will be with you every step in case of an emergency."

If confronting my not-quite-ready-for-adulthood children with death options was not enough, Michael began suggesting we basically needed to boot them out of the nest completely. A suggestion he made months earlier became more frequent and determined. *To put our home up for sale.*

"You really think we have to sell our house?" I looked at the realtors' business cards spread out on the kitchen table.

"We need to be all in, hon. Who knows how long we will be gone? It would be too much to ask someone to take care of the house for us. Plus, maintaining the mortgage means we'd have to raise more money."

Selling the house troubled me. John had returned to live with us after a one-year college run on the East Coast which hadn't gone as well as planned, and Anna needed a place to spend her college breaks.

Just as I was gearing up to basically issue a keeping-the-house ultimatum, something unexpected took place.

A couple from our church walked up to Michael at church on Sunday. "Mike, this has never happened to us before." The wife spoke first. "But last week, I sensed clearly that God was leading us to pay your house payment while you're in Kabul."

"And I sensed the same thing," continued the husband looking excitedly at Michael. "Though we'd not talked about it before. We are sure this is what God wants us to do."

My husband is more comfortable giving than receiving, but he could not dismiss such a divine occurrence and refuse their offer. "You have no idea how this blesses my family. Thank you," was all he could manage to reply.

When Michael reported the amazing event to me that night, my mother's heart flooded with peace. I simultaneously wept and clapped in gratitude.

Not only was one major financial burden lifted, and my children provided for, but I soon learned there would be no need to fundraise further. Oasis was awarded a grant in spring 2005, turning KIA into the International School of Kabul (ISK). Since Michael had agreed to work at the school too, we both had salaries!

During the upcoming holidays, many of our extended family in Oklahoma and Virginia vocalized their concerns about our plan to relocate to a war zone. We tried to assuage their fears for our safety, but I wasn't a strong salesperson, still experiencing my own doubt and anxiety.

With the direct gaze and firm voice I knew so well from my time as a strong-willed child and challenging teenager, my dad spoke to me in December 2004 following Sarah's Missouri wedding reception. "I'm shocked you would leave your kids and go to such a dangerous place. What if something happens to you? What's your plan?" I sighed. Michael knew to remain silent in this father-daughter exchange.

Squeezing my hands in my lap, I listed our personal preparations. Just as he required when I asked permission for an outing with friends in high school, I gave details about our safety and the agenda for our time away—as much as I could at that point anyway.

Never taking his brown eyes from my matching ones, he listened carefully. His expression changed from a fierce lion's to a loving, concerned father's. I knew all the facets of my dad's parenting and more than that, I knew he trusted my judgment. But he would do his best to contribute to wise planning by asking hard questions.

"All right then. We will pray for you. I respect you both for making this choice to do what you believe God is asking of you." A slight nod of his head and discussion over. *Whew.* I wiped my sweaty hands on my pant legs.

My in-laws plied us with similar questions, tearfully and without the interrogation overtones. "Will you be safe over there? We're worried you won't return. What about Sarah, John, and Anna? Aren't they scared for you to leave?" This is the parenting that clearly contributed to my husband being a feeling responder over a thinker. I let him handle the answers this time. Afghanistan was his idea, after all.

In the weeks leading up to our departure, in the dark and quiet of our bedroom, I'd listen to Michael's gentle snoring and gaze heavenward with questions pouring out to God. *What if I didn't come to love Afghanistan or its people? Could I pull off this administrator job? Would I have any friends outside of the workplace with whom I could take off my leader hat? Would my children be okay on their own at such a young age? Are you sure, God, this is the right choice?*

We'd been preparing for the worst and doing our best to think everything through with the help of others who cared deeply for us. All of my big worries stateside had been taken care of by no actions I'd taken on my own, and we'd been given extraordinary provision. None of my remaining fears about our future would be answered this side of Kabul.

A new season for me and my husband had begun, even if I secretly wished it was happening to someone else.

It was time to go. I was ready...I hoped.

The Unveiled Truth: I try to consider all of the 'what ifs' in my life plans and prepare for the unknown. But the unknown remains the unknown.

When anxiety grabs hold of us, there's no shame in admitting it. We should talk it out with those who matter most. Problem solve as best we can, pray, cry, and listen to counsel.

After you've prepared for the worst, choose to hope for the best. For there's no quicker way to sabotage progress than to lose faith in the face of a new day and new possibilities.

How should you be preparing for upcoming, unknown future events?

3

The Pain of Obedience

In late July 2005, I adjusted my headscarf and climbed out of a vehicle onto the dusty, unpaved Kabul street, lined with walled properties that would become home for the school and staff. There were few trees and little grass. I felt a mixture of relief and shock. Relief that the days of international travel and the chaos of the Kabul airport were over. Shock that this was it and I was here.

"Here we are again, whoot-whoot!" Two women who were seasoned short-term workers in Afghanistan from our St. Joseph church high-fived each other. They'd graciously come to help us get settled into our campus apartment while Michael and I joined the ISK team to get the school up and running.

Our kids, John and Anna, also stepped out of the vehicle and stood staring at the eight-foot, white, painted concrete walls. We thought it might help them to see where their parents would be serving and had brought them along. Anna still strongly resisted our plan, but we hoped after this trip she might eventually adopt a less dramatic, more reasonable attitude about the whole thing.

"Yay, the Goolsbys are here!" I turned to see one of the teachers I'd met on my visit to the school a year ago. She came out of one of the many colorful metal security gates in the line of walls and cheerfully greeted our kids and friends. "Let me take you guys to your apartment." She grabbed a couple of suitcases and led the way through a different colored gate into a marble-covered courtyard with three buildings inside a walled yard.

"This is the Marble Mansion for the single female teachers." Our guide nodded in the direction of the attractive three-story structure ahead of us. "And your apartment is across the patio on this side. Another ISK couple will take the apartment next door. They are freshly painted and ready."

After dropping our luggage inside the small downstairs, our friendly helper began to exit. "Come to the Marble Mansion for some cereal and boxed milk for your breakfast tomorrow. We'll bring in kebabs later for everyone's supper." She let the screen door slap sharply behind her.

The six of us in our group stood frozen in the small, empty dining room, the females dripping sweat in our wrist-to-ankle coverings and headscarves. Even in short sleeves, Michael and John were uncomfortable and moved to open what windows there were to get air circulating.

Our two friends decided to take their bags over to the Marble Mansion where there were open beds until all the teachers arrived. They wisely determined to allow us to share the limited apartment space with our children for the few days we had together.

"Can I take this scarf off and put on a t-shirt and shorts?" Anna finally spoke. Her red face and tired eyes mirrored my own misery.

"Honey, you don't have to wear your scarf inside our house, but you can't put on shorts." I apologetically took her hand as I delivered this bad news. "John, you can't either. Afghans consider shorts like underwear. I'm sorry. I know it is awful without air conditioning in this heat." My eyes searched Anna's face for some sign of positive response.

None. She followed John up the narrow cement stairs to the bedrooms, peeling off her scarf. "Can you believe this place?" I heard her mutter to her brother as they disappeared from view.

Michael and I exchanged fatigued, sad glances. He moved the luggage away from the door. "I will find some fans and get John to tack sheets over the windows for makeshift curtains. Anna can put on shorts as long as she stays inside and no male workers need to come in to fix anything." He lightly patted my shoulder as he went out the door. "It will be okay."

Plopping down onto a plastic patio chair, the only furniture in the tiny kitchen, I let out a long sigh. I was too hot and tired to cry. I certainly did not feel like the new principal of the most prestigious school in Afghanistan, the newly renamed International School of Kabul (ISK), due to open in a few short weeks. I took a deep breath for courage. *I only signed up for two years. The time will probably fly by quickly with so much to do.*

I knew a troop of dedicated, highly trained educational professionals were joining me in the work, or I would never have come. Just a month ago, we had spent two weeks with ISK's staff in Pre-Field Orientation (PFO) at the Oasis headquarters in Southaven, MS. This helped us get acquainted and understand more about the variety of students we would be instructing and how we could successfully navigate culture adaptation.

Of the team, only my new boss, Dr. Byron Greene, the recently hired *male* school director, Michael, and I had ever previously traveled to Kabul. However, many on the team had impressive stories about their own calling to Afghanistan. Though some were more adventure-seekers than educators, looking for a once-in-a-lifetime experience, all were willing to work hard with energy and enthusiasm.

"I knew ten years ago that I wanted to work in Afghanistan, when a medical worker spoke at my church," one team member had told me at PFO. "I can't wait to finally get there."

Another shared shyly in her Georgia-Arkansas accent how she had been rejected by some organizations to work in Afghanistan due to past emotional and physical issues. "I was so excited to be accepted by Oasis to help start the school. I love to teach math, and I know how to get students to love it, too!"

At PFO, the ISK team enjoyed celebrity status among the other teachers departing to Oasis schools around the world. Not only were we headed into a high-risk project, but we were the largest team in attendance that year. The special attention at PFO had worked magic on my attitude while I was still in the U.S., but fell painfully short upon my entrance into Kabul reality.

During our first in-country week, staff arrived day by day, and ISK meetings lasted morning till afternoon. Our two friends took John and Anna all over the hot, crowded city gathering dishes, towels, furniture, and rugs to make our small apartment more like a home. These ladies knew how to shop, bartering with the best of Kabul's shopkeepers to stretch the set-up funds that caring individuals and our hometown church had given us.

"These Afghan guys are getting to me," John confessed as he lay before the fan to cool off. The four shoppers had been out all day in the enduring Kabul sunshine and suffocating crowds. "I literally pushed myself in front of this one man who kept staring at Anna while trying to get closer to her. What is their deal with staring at women?"

I shook my head, having no explanation for this irritating habit. No woman appreciates being stared at, but the staring in Afghanistan, and in many other countries in that area of the world, was worse than we'd ever encountered. Western men were just as uncomfortable with the amount of staring and often stepped between the women and the offenders in a protective, chivalrous way.

On our children's last night in Kabul, we were invited to meet with the mayor at the InterContinental Hotel. Anna's stomach was upset, so I stayed back in the ISK apartment while the others went without us. I hoped the alone time would give me an opportunity to find out if her thoughts about Afghanistan and our decision to come had changed.

"So, Anna, what was your favorite part of this visit?" I asked as I sat on the bed beside her where the fan was directed. She had her eyes partly closed, looking up at the ceiling.

Her silence filled the hot, still airspace.

I brushed her bangs off her sweaty forehead and stroked her arm lightly, waiting.

Rolling over to her side to look at me, she quietly said, "No offense, Mom, but there is nothing about this place I like, except for the work you and Dad plan to do to help the people."

Ouch. I wished I had some reassuring words to counter her assessment, but instead, my own words to Michael upon examining his first Afghanistan trip photos flooded my thoughts. *This is no place to live, not for a woman, not for me.* So far, in my short time of Kabul exposure in 2004 and this week, I was not able to completely change my own negative viewpoint.

I suffered endless male stares every time I walked on a Kabul street, even with the required male escort, just like she did during the week's shopping trips to the crowded marketplace. The food was unfamiliar and not flavorful to my palette—from the boxed milk to the flat, chewy bread. The campus and our school apartment were not comfortable, aesthetic places yet. There was no air conditioning or even nighttime electricity to run a fan, only noisy, diesel-smelling, expensive generators we ran from six-thirty am to eleven pm. There were no sidewalks or paved roads, or even a McDonalds, and hardly any English spoken outside the school compound.

I truthfully felt the same way as Anna but said nothing. I kissed her warm, sweet cheek and looked into her beautiful brown eyes with tenderness and acceptance. Perhaps this trip hadn't done anything to change her opinion of us moving out here. Maybe it had only made it worse.

However, John was having a great time.

When returning from their dinner outing, I could hear John and our friends chatting in the courtyard. Their cheery conversation and laughter floated up to our open apartment window. As Michael and John entered the apartment downstairs, I heard him say to his dad, "I think I'll ask my political science advisor if I can do my internship in Kabul next semester. Could I stay in your other bedroom? There are some people in the international community doing amazing things here who would be great to work with."

Like father, like son. His upbeat plan made me smile—and hope.

When our friends and children left the next day, I vacillated between wanting to hide away in my apartment with my heartache or scream at Michael for bringing this awful separation into my life. I never wanted to be apart from my family and friends or my American life. What if I didn't come to love this place or the people, or even to appreciate it at all?

Oh, if only this was happening to someone else, and I was leaving on the airplane with John and Anna. *Are you listening, God? I'm hurting.*

With so little privacy, my options were limited to fully expressing the depth of my pain. I desperately needed a distraction or I worried I might lose it in a public, ugly way. So, I pushed my feelings down and hoped the work facing me would help bury my anxiety. We stayed focused the next week from eight in the morning until five in the evening, crafting ISK vision statements and core values using team building activities. These pioneering activities engaged me and helped buoy my feelings. In fact, once we started enrolling students, I was nearly too busy to even think about myself.

"Please, miss, can my children come to this school?" I heard this question over and over throughout the weeks of August and into September.

Without any formal advertising, families were lining up for a chance at something better than the sub-standard Afghan school environment. Everyone in the national and international community seemed to know about the new American school. People came daily to find out how to get their children admitted.

"We are going to pass the 150 mark easily," my administrative assistant Karen reported cheerfully a couple of weeks into our enrollment. She piled more student applications on my desk. "Where are we going to put all these kids?" Our classrooms weren't much more than small, converted house bedrooms. "They just keep calling and coming in. Isn't it great?"

I watched her leave and envied the bounce in her steps.

Most of the staff were thrilled at having a role in this ground-breaking endeavor, but I was secretly embarrassed by not being able to chime in with their ecstatic sentiments. Though I was their leader, my heart was divided, wanting to be back home in Missouri but also wanting to fulfill my commitment at ISK.

In bed alongside Michael in the pitch-dark silence of those summer Kabul nights, I felt miserable and alone. My husband loved his third-world home and the daily challenges of working construction without much experience in renovations. He especially enjoyed his time with his team of Afghan maintenance men who followed him around morning to evening.

I thought You were calling me here, God. But when will the joy of obedience hit me? Or will this pain of family separation and uncomfortable, primitive surroundings last for two whole years? I don't think I can stand it.

At a weekly Friday service in early September, at the only international church for foreign Christians allowed in Kabul, I closed my eyes to focus on my faith. Familiar worship lyrics sung by the varying international accents in our mixed congregation soothed me. In this little Kabul church, global workers from all over the UK, Finland, New Zealand, Germany, Canada, France, Netherlands, South Africa, Tajikistan, India,

China, Argentina, Korea, and beyond gathered to worship the same God.

It wasn't just me alone, struggling to do God's will here. No, I was part of a larger movement, a larger church family. With my eyes closed, I imagined this group playing out the scene in Revelation 7:9 (NIV): *After this I looked, and there before me was a great multitude that no one could count, from every nation, tribe, people and language, standing before the throne and before the Lamb. They were wearing white robes and were holding palm branches in their hands.*

I felt myself miraculously lifting out of my small pit of woes and worries. Not completely, but like a cool breeze of restoration, the words sung by the people around me who'd come together for the same purpose encouraged my wearied soul.

God was doing something big here in Afghanistan.

I'd been invited to be a part, and I was clearly *not* alone. There were others, so many others, right here and more back home, who'd joined in with their hearts and prayers to work alongside me.

Though moist, I opened my eyes. I wanted to change my attitude. I wanted to feel differently. I offered myself anew to God and to Afghanistan. *I am here for this time, for your purposes. I don't want to miss anything by letting pain win.*

God seemed to whisper to my desperate and fearful spirit: *I am here with you. I led you this far, and I am not leaving you. I will care for those you have left behind. I will care for you and walk beside you in this journey. I will guide you in your new job. You can trust me. Have I ever failed you?*

No. God had never failed me. Confused me. Challenged me. Let me make mistakes. But never left me. I walked back to our apartment from the service on wobbly legs but moving forward with new determination and renewed hope that the heartache over missing my children and former life would soon lessen.

The Unveiled Truth: I am a rule-follower type who believes in the general good of trusting and obeying, even when painful. Exercise, childbirth, final exams, house cleaning, and troubled relationships are just some of the things that have brought me pain. But when I persevered, I gained a reward in the end.

When our hearts choose to focus on the pain, we diminish the positive outcomes that are possible once the task is completed. We do well to focus on the goal and obey God in His leading. Doing so doesn't erase the pain of the trial, but we don't have to let pain derail us either.

There is a prize for obedience, though not always obvious or immediate. Push through the pain and you'll almost always be glad you did.

What difficulties are sidetracking you from completing a God-given task?

4

The Precious Pearl of Education

"My three children attend school in New Jersey." An Afghan-American father handed me official transcripts and grade cards. "Now I have a good job with the U.S. military here and want to bring them to Afghanistan. Please, can they come to your school?" Brown eyes searched my face for affirmation.

A large percentage of ISK students with Afghan ethnicity carried Canadian or U.S. passports. I tried to accommodate these Western students as this was their best school option. They breathed a sigh of relief when I told them they would not have to attend the local schools where their jeans and athletic shoes would be foreign and their Dari (national academic language) too weak to succeed in the classroom.

"Yes, yes, English good. They take English classes two years," promised a local Afghan father handing me a handwritten grade report in Dari. “Give them test. You see. They go to ISK?” More brown eyes pled for my approval.

Families and students from all over Kabul plus sixteen other countries appeared for weeks in August and even into September after the school opened. They all wanted to be admitted to ISK.

“How many grade levels are we testing today?” I daily waded through the crowd of students and parents in the admin building foyer to reach my assistant’s desk.

Ever-efficient Karen whipped out her spreadsheet and lists. “Since we pulled K-2 non-English speakers out of testing, not so many today, thankfully. Here you go.”

I balanced the stack of our American standardized admission tests in reading comprehension and math and led the group downstairs to a large classroom outfitted with Western style desks. As a seasoned school counselor and no one in that role at ISK, I handled the testing. To determine what grade level to even assess felt like rolling the dice and hoping for the right number. Birthdays were vague and often arbitrarily assigned by low-level government workers or parents with no official birth records.

“My son is first in his class.” I heard this boast from almost every local parent wanting to enroll his child at ISK. We learned early on that principals and headmasters could be paid to give this ranking to students. Stamped and signed Afghan school reports offered little clarity with only *passed* or one letter grade representing an entire year of coursework.

After scoring the half-day assessments, Karen would give me her best guess on either acceptance and grade placement or rejection. We looked at parental profiles to see how committed and English-able they would be to help their children. Also, was there available space in the grade being considered for admission? How many siblings wanted admission?

For borderline students, I passed out the applications to select teachers and administrative members. "Help me make these decisions. We can't take all these older, non-English speaking students. The little ones up to about grade two can learn phonics with their classmates and pick up English quickly. But we need to keep the standards as close as possible to each grade level since we're going for U.S. accreditation. We can't help everyone, right?"

"Whoa, this guy wants to be in fourth grade, but he's already twelve? He probably has facial hair," remarked my seasoned fourth-grade instructor who taught for years in Africa before coming to Kabul. "I know Afghan schools go by years of schooling, not birthdate, but we have to have some boundaries." She pulled two older student applications from her stack and gave them to me, shaking her head no.

I took the rejected applications back and frowned. Should I give every earnest young person (or pushy parent) a chance to learn at the best school in the country? What other educational options did they have?

There were many new public Afghan school buildings, thanks to generous countries around the world, but nothing much inside, no libraries or science labs or even enough desks, books, or blackboards. Private Afghan schools were popping up with business sponsors to help with the massive illiteracy problems but also to make money. The lack of qualified teachers after years of war and fleeing Afghan citizens added to the overall education problem.

All ISK teachers were degreed and properly credentialed,

some with master's degrees. They might be fresh out of college or with years of instructional history, but they all wanted to do their best for the students coming to ISK. They hoped to make a difference in this desperate country, just like I did.

Despite gathering input from my experienced, talented ISK staff, the final decision was left to me. Principals in Afghan culture carry a lot of power and receive much respect, even if female. It was overwhelming and taxing.

Alone in the admin building at the end of another full day, I gazed out the window in my office, feeling heavy and tired. *Would the teacher of that class be overwhelmed with such a large range of abilities or would she or he be able to handle it? Would the family support the student in homework and study time at home to catch up to grade level if I give them this chance? Would I be making political and important people upset by rejecting certain students? Would the family be able to pay their tuition?*

After reviewing all the data, I tried to determine a wise, compassionate, and reasonable judgment for each student, knowing I would be called upon to defend my decision. Not a favorite part of my new job.

"Here are the happy calls." The next day, I handed Karen one stack of admission forms. "And here are the firm no's." I placed another stack on her desk. "And this is the 'come back next year with more English acquisition and apply again' pile."

Karen nodded as she organized the three piles and consulted her spreadsheet for phone numbers. I didn't envy her task of making these calls, but she was superb at delivering the messages and not accepting pushback. Though that didn't stop the excluded parents from making unannounced campus visits to argue with her and me.

Filling the classrooms with students was only part of the

looming task. Filling them with supplies and furniture was a whole other problem.

"Our Pakistani desks, tables, chairs, and office furniture are being held at the border," we heard from one of our Afghan staff in an admin meeting in late August. "They want us to pay bribes like everyone else to get them released to us."

"No!" Byron slapped his desk. "We're not playing that game. Let the stuff sit there. Bribes are not in our budget and that is not the way we are going to do things, no matter what the culture deems normal."

"Okay. I will deliver that message and see what I can do," our Afghan teammate left with his cell phone to try and work magic while we brainstormed what to use for classrooms still needing desks and tables and chairs. We ordered traditional toshaks (large stuffed pillows present in every Afghan home for sitting and sleeping) for the younger grades from a local tailor and purchased used school furniture wherever we could find it.

ISK was slowly evolving into a school, but still not like any I had ever worked in before. I wished for more for my team and the coming students. Just like a wife and mother wants her home to be an inviting, inspiring place for her family, as the principal, I wanted ISK to be a wonderful place to learn and work for my people.

I was elated that help was on the way.

While at Pre-Field Orientation in June, Byron and I spent hours with Oasis staff ordering curriculum and school supplies. As seasoned school leaders, we had a solid idea what was essential. Oasis invited FedEx, headquartered in nearby Memphis, to support the ISK project. They deeply discounted our seven-ton shipment from the States that arrived in stages over the weeks of August. Textbooks, computers, and all manner of school supplies purchased at Wal-Mart and U.S. teacher stores made up most of the shipment.

"It's like Christmas," one of the staff remarked to me as she grabbed two tubs from the first FedEx shipment that finally arrived. "Now I can do the bulletin boards in my classroom!"

Smiling and grabbing a stack of whiteboards off the pile to take inside, I doubted most educators showed as much enthusiasm about their job as my first-grade teacher fresh from her California college. Especially in a place like Afghanistan. Made me proud to head such a team of dedicated professionals.

"Order a set for every elementary class." I handed the local carpenter's drawings for student cubbies to Karen one day between student interviews. "They will fit in the foyers outside the classrooms. We still need lockers for the secondary building. Where can we find them in Kabul?"

She shook her head, but I knew Karen's strong strategic mind was already thinking of parents and workmen to check with.

Getting the buildings ready required something beyond patience. Byron handled most of the decisions for the property improvements along with Michael as the ISK Operations Manager and a few other team members. Nothing happened quickly as we tried to create our version of a school with unfamiliar materials and house-foundations. Teachers wanted to get their rooms ready for students, but walls were being moved or repaired and workmen took up hall space with equipment.

"You look really beat," I remarked to Michael as I glanced at the clock which read seven o'clock. "Did you get dinner in the dining hall?"

"Too tired to eat," he replied and flopped across our bed. In mere seconds, I heard him softly snoring.

Michael and his Afghan maintenance team labored ten to twelve hours per day trying to open the school on time. It was painful to see the antiquated tools used by workmen and the length of time it took his crew to finish seemingly simple tasks. The mess made by careless workers took as long to clean up as the actual renovation process.

It was a stressful time for everyone as we watched the days flying by and no closer to opening ISK by late August. We pushed back the start date to September which made for bored teachers and phone calls from waiting, eager students.

To cope with the daily problems and constant delays, we turned to laughter to lighten the load since we had limited access to the outside world.

We were fortunate to have many ISK team members who regularly delivered jokes and puns over meals in the staff dining room and supplied funny videos to share in the Marble Mansion's recreation room on nights and weekends.

One of the most witty and fun-loving staff members was a young Afghan man named Khalid. He was a true asset to ISK with his dual language abilities, salesmanship, bartering skills, and cultural translations. He became a special help to me as principal to navigate government and cultural issues and is still a friend today.

His positive outlook and natural sense of humor made hard times more bearable. He enjoyed sharing Persian proverbs with me and I tried to explain English language idioms to him. This proved hilarious at times and a great stress reliever.

"Be careful now, Khalid, you know what they say, *the walls have ears*," I cautioned as he began talking about one of our new ISK father's questionable reputation. I motioned him to follow me into my office.

As he closed the door behind him, he said, "Walls have ears? No, we say it this way: *Walls have mice, and mice have ears.* That makes more sense, does it not?" I had to nod my head in agreement. He clapped his hands and smiled in victory.

Another time I tried to explain a decision I made as we rode through the crowded Kabul streets for a Ministry of Education appointment. "I thought it through, but since *the buck stops with me*, I just had to say no." I looked to see if Khalid understood.

"Oh, yes, I know about this *kicking the bucket* that you speak of." We turned into the Ministry checkpoint and showed our identification to the guard.

"What? No, wait, that is not what I'm saying at all!" I responded between giggles. The driver parked the car and we headed past the concrete bomb barriers and into the government building. As we walked the hallways, I tried to explain that the saying Harry Truman made popular had nothing to do with hanging people from a tree while standing on a bucket. Makes me chuckle even now.

Khalid's masterpieces, however, were practical jokes plotted and superbly executed. He loved to involve my husband, also a big fan of funny business. In the August renovation process, Byron's office needed repainting and he was particular about style and appearance. He noticed the strange color choices the local painters deemed appropriate, so he delivered firm directions to Michael and Khalid on the chosen shade for his office and then left for a trip out of Kabul.

Several days later, I heard Khalid calling down the stairs in the admin building. "Oh, no! This is not good at all! Mister Mike, please come right away."

My husband took the marble steps two at a time to join Khalid inside Byron's office. I quickly joined them in curiosity and immediately saw the trouble.

"What happened to the off-white color Byron picked for the workers to use?" Michael asked as he noted the lavender glow of the large, sunny room. "This will not go over well, not at all."

I had to nod vigorously in agreement.

Panic was replaced by mischief when the two men envisioned Byron's outrage at this feminine-looking director's office. Our boss from Georgia considered himself quite the outdoorsy, man's man with hunting and camping as his favorite pastimes. The Afghan culture of men holding hands and embracing, even kissing cheeks in greeting, left him cringing and embarrassed.

When I heard Khalid say, "I have an idea, Mister Mike." I shook my finger at the two of them.

"You better behave yourselves," I said. But somehow, I knew they wouldn't. However, I had a feeling it would be highly entertaining for the rest of us. I asked nothing more so I could claim innocence when things went down.

The two pranksters hurried into town and collected an impressive array of office accessories such as a wastebasket and alarm clock, and even personal items like soap and towels, all in various bright shades of *pink*. In Afghanistan, it is common to see men wearing these colors in shirts, ties, and the traditional shalwar kameez, a loose pant outfit with a tunic top reaching below the knees. But most Western men, especially Byron, held a much different opinion of wearing pastel hues.

"Read this masterpiece." My husband handed me a card the next day.

Khalid stood right beside him, grinning and snickering. I read out loud the original poem, dedicated to declaring Byron's true love of pink playing off his last name green.

"You know he will hit the roof, right?" I tried to give the grown-but-childlike men in front of my desk my most stern principal look. They nodded eagerly. Clearly Byron hitting the roof was the goal. I handed the poem back and shooed them away.

They placed the anonymous note in the box of pretty pink things and prominently placed it on Byron's desk in the lavender office. Word spread to the team. Many of the staff gathered in the administration building the morning Byron was due to return to campus.

"What is everybody doing?" Byron asked as he entered and saw the crowd. He looked at me. "Why are all these people in the admin building and not working?"

I shrugged my shoulders, walked with him upstairs, and waited outside while he unlocked his office door.

The silence lasted only a second. "Khalid! Michael! What happened to my office? Get up here now!" The marble floors of the admin building amplified the shouting deliciously for the two pranksters.

Laughter broke out all over the building from the library to the workroom to the IT offices. Byron did not disappoint us in his long-winded ranting and raving over the paint color and feminine accessories.

"Were you in on this, too?" He glared at me.

"Not me," I innocently replied as I left the now-infamous lavender office. I saluted Khalid and Michael as they sheepishly entered the scene of the crime. This elaborate stunt was the perfect stress-buster, and we all benefitted from the humor therapy.

The staff laughed for days as we retold the joke, although not in Byron's presence. Khalid and Michael got the office quickly repainted, the correct color, and I was given the unappreciated girly gifts. Over the next seven years, every time I looked at the pink alarm clock in my ISK campus apartment, I smiled in remembrance of the prank.

ISK finally opened on September 5, 2005. We celebrated with two open-house events, inviting U.S. Ambassador Ronald E. Neumann and other U.S. and Afghan public figures that supported our venture. With no auditorium or indoor assembly space, we rented chairs, toshaks, carpets, and tents in various shades of Afghan red. This created a wildly colorful event in the yard behind the admin building. There was an elevated back porch resembling a stage for the speakers to use with microphones. None of the Afghan attendees thought anything unusual about our outdoor theater because local weddings and family reunions used the same resources.

Before leaving America, knowing we could not have a public billboard or towering ISK street sign for security reasons, I had the idea to make some banners. One said, "New Beginnings 2005...International School of Kabul." Another said, "Building a Better World, One Student at a Time." These were hung above the entrance of the admin building and one at the gate into our walled compound where cars would drop off students.

Over the schoolyard entrance, Khalid had a worker paint a motto that he liked: "Every day in every way, better and better."

"Hmm, do you know where this saying comes from, Khalid?" I turned from the finished doorway project to look at his proud face.

"No, do you? I just heard a foreign friend say it, and I think it gives hope about the future of my country. Which ISK is helping us improve. It's good, right?" He looked at me expecting another English idiom lesson.

Knowing this was actually a line from a vintage movie about a character in a mental hospital, I smiled at his enthusiasm, patted his shoulder in approval, and walked down the dusty street to the admin building. I decided to let it remain.

Education does have the potential to make every day better, and that is one thing Afghanistan needs desperately.

Those weeks of creating a school from almost nothing, with delays and disappointments, taught us lessons about teamwork, flexibility, adaptation, grace for mistakes, and the power of humor and positive attitudes.

With much to learn ahead of us, even for those of us who were seasoned educators, we opened our doors to a whole new world of international education and culture, new to us and new to Afghanistan.

The Unveiled Truth: I have never regretted my career choice of education and all the forms of it I have experienced in my lifetime.

We all have wisdom, knowledge, skills, and experiences to share with others that can enrich our own lives in the exchange. And we always have more to learn from others, even outside the classroom, if we choose to be receptive and engage the world as students of people and culture. Education and learning are precious gifts for all of us.

No matter your age, your past, or your seemingly limited resources and opportunities, determine to learn new things.

Education makes the future so much richer, so much more interesting.

And if you haven't already...you should learn to laugh.

How can you incorporate more learning, either academically or experientially, in your life?

5

Lift Up Your Eyes

Gazing out of the window on my first airplane trip to Afghanistan in 2004, I'd thought the scenery depressing. The decades of war, the desperate need for heating fuel, the years of drought, and the desert climate all contributed to the missing trees and grass. *It is all so drab, so lifeless. Where is the green in all this khaki? Yuck.*

The dusty, colorless environment fit my overall mood those first few months after my arrival in 2005. But with the campus slowly taking place, classrooms decorated by creative teachers, and the attractive furniture finally released from the customs imprisonment (with no ransom paid) and wonderful Afghan carpets filling staff housing, delightful aesthetics began to appear.

"Where did you get all these geraniums, Ali?" I bent to investigate the collection of bright red, pink, and white blooms in the three dozen pots in the admin courtyard. We were preparing the campus for our first Open House event.

Ali was one of our older Afghan staff and the designated gardener. "Good to grow," he told me in his broken English while pinching off the withered bits of each plant. He motioned to the flower box by my office window with a questioning look.

"Yes, yes, please. I would love to have flowers planted there." I excitedly chose six healthy red and white geraniums, my favorite combination. I thanked Ali and entered the admin building with a smile of gratitude. Such a small thing, beautiful flowers, but as a gardener myself and missing my home plants, so appreciated. Along with geraniums, Ali kept roses in full display around our compound from spring to November. Such a mystery that these vibrant, blooming bushes rose out of the dusty ground without special attention.

When the rain came, the billowing dust turned to sticky mud. The mess was worse than the dust, but the rains brought relief through cleaner air. I could actually see vibrant color on trees and plants when the showers removed the dusty camouflage. But only briefly, as the high desert sun dried the ground quickly and the dust always returned.

"So much dust everywhere. I have never washed my hands so much in my life, have you?" I asked Michael as he returned to our campus apartment after a long day of maintenance management.

"Aren't you glad to have help with the housecleaning?" He removed his shoes at the door as culturally expected, helpful also for keeping dirt out of the apartment. "I came home this afternoon to shut all the windows during the dust storm. Doesn't keep it out completely, though. Nadia will have to clean again tomorrow." We both noticed the fine film covering our new dining room table and shrugged our shoulders. Dust was pervasive.

Ah, but out of the dust rose...the mountains.

Like Denver, Kabul has several mountain ranges encircling it. They weren't tree-covered like the Appalachians or Ozarks, or mighty granite peaks like the Rockies, but they were majestic in their own way. Walking down the dusty ISK street, I would lift my eyes to see the sunny blue skies outlining the mountains on every side and feel momentarily pleased with my surroundings. Sunrise and sunset photos over the hills were popular postings by staff on social media and undeniably breathtaking. Many fit foreigners loved to hike the stark inclines of Kabul's mountains.

I myself took advantage of the natural beauty for exercise. I love to walk, but in Afghanistan, even that took much planning.

"Five-thirty? Are you kidding? Why so early?" I quizzed Karen as she related the next morning's departure plan. Interested team members could start their Thursday/Friday weekend by climbing aboard the school's fifteen passenger van for outdoor exercise at Qargha Lake, a nearby recreation spot, quite different from dirty Kabul.

"If we want to enjoy jogging or walking around the lake without drawing crowds of males staring at us, we have to go early." She took the stack of team memos to distribute around campus. "We'll be back in time for a great breakfast courtesy of the women in the Marble Mansion."

Michael and I pulled our weary bodies out of bed in the semi-darkness the next day and boarded the van with the other, mostly younger, staff. Unpolluted air, lake views, and open spaces drew us more than extended sleep. Kabul's bowl-like situation encompassed by the mountains kept air from circulating. With the overload of diesel fuel, unregulated burning of anything, uncovered sewer drainage, and garbage smells everywhere, my eyes and nose longed for fresh air.

"Look at that sign." Michael pointed out the van window to a hand-painted banner at the entrance to the Qargha Lake area. We both laughed, as did the whole van, at the quizzical sight that announced *Kabul Gulf Cours*.

"Can't we take off our headscarves, Khalid?" I asked on behalf of the ready-to-run female teachers after we climbed out of the van. We were already sweltering in thigh-long tunics covering jeans, long sleeves, and scarves. "No one's here this early to see us being culturally inappropriate."

With his trademark charm, Khalid grinned. "Tell you what, ladies. Next time, I shall wear shorts, which you know is shocking here. That way, everyone will be so focused on me, they will not notice missing headscarves."

Involuntarily smiling at Khalid's diplomatic response, we repositioned our scarves, tucking them in or winding them farther around our necks, sighed, and pushed onward around the lake. Michael and I took the slower gravel path, and with the absence of peering eyes, held hands, inhaled the unpolluted air, and watched the sun rise over the blue water as we walked.

"This is nice. You can almost forget where you are, don't you think?" Michael asked after a few relaxing moments of silence and privacy.

Easy for you to say, in your short sleeves and scarf-less head. I wisely left those words unspoken to keep from ruining the moment. If I was going to survive, no, thrive in this strange and often uncomfortable place that was now my home, then I must welcome the beauty, the peace, the wonder, the goodness that was available to embrace. I looked at my husband and smiled.

The Kabul chaos bothered me far more than bombs and guns, which were real threats, but not my daily challenge. Living in an overcrowded, unorganized city was draining to a lifelong suburban dweller like me.

Kabul was originally planned for about 250-300,000 people, but in 2005, it became home to over four million, mostly returning refugees. The list of problems resulting from this overcrowding included not enough roads, water, electricity, schools, or access to health care. Basic housing for the nationals proved insufficient, and I watched mud dwellings move up the mountainsides where no one seemed to own the land.

Contrast those too few resources with too many taxis, bicycles, pedestrians, beggars, flocks of goats and sheep (with their droppings), and horse-drawn carts all vying for the same walk and roadway space. Traffic was crazy with few yellow lines or stoplights. Drivers went where they liked, even in the opposite lane, confronting the coming stream of vehicles until somebody gave way.

New restaurants, cafes, and larger stores popped up on the Kabul scene regularly, but they were not kin to anything familiar I left behind in the States. Finding a decent cup of coffee in a country of tea drinkers or a good ol'American hamburger was almost impossible.

"I can't believe it! Fritos!" I exclaimed in delight to a teammate while shopping at a foreigner-friendly shop one day. When the shopkeeper told me the price of those date-expired chips, my eyes widened. "Five dollars? Unbelievable. I already paid seven for a case of Diet Coke." I bought them anyway and limited my daily intake to make the treasure last as long as possible.

In the early Kabul years, I made my own share of trips off

campus, wading through the crowds and trying to locate what I needed with few visible English signs to help. I had to gear up for the upcoming onslaught to my senses and mobs of people everywhere. But not all the effort was stressful. At a plastics shop near ISK, I made friends with the one-armed, friendly owner.

"Salaam Alaikum." He bowed toward me in respect and waved me into his crowded shop. It was reminiscent of an old-fashioned Woolworths or Ben Franklin 5&10 Store, stacked with vast, seemingly random housewares from floor to ceiling. He spoke almost no English but delighted to show me his newest acquisitions each visit.

I loved to look around at his collection. When I had trouble finding bowls big enough to hold full batches of popcorn, he took on the challenge to locate them for me. A week later, he proudly waved me into his shop. At first, he acted like the large pink plastic bowls were a gift and would not take any money. I learned this is a facet of Afghan hospitality, to give a desired item to a guest, especially a foreigner. "*Ne, ne*," I persisted, but made sure he knew I was thankful for his find. "*Tashakor*."

He continued to persist, but I finally got his young relative assistant to tell me the price. I handed over the *Afghanis* (Afghan currency) and asked him to communicate to the owner that I was the honored one to have met such an excellent businessman and new friend. I waved goodbye as I left the shop.

One October morning that first year in Kabul, I heard Michael call to me as I got ready for work. "Gail, come see this."

I stepped outside, noticed the white powder on our marble patio courtyard, and then looked up.

Wow. My mouth fell open.

When I saw that first autumn snowfall on the many peaks surrounding Kabul, I was enraptured. The transformation from a dusty, bland city was powerful. The sparkling white frosting on the brown mountain tops made a picturesque contrast. As a December birthday girl, I have always loved snow and yearly hoped it would appear as a special gift on my day. Now, it served to lift my spirits even higher, to remind me again, that God was present and able to enter any bleakness in wonderfully personal ways.

The Unveiled Truth: In my opinion, Kabul and Afghanistan would not qualify as scenic nor make a pretty postcard. Some staff even experienced a type of seasonal depression at the lack of color in the natural surroundings. But when I purposely opened my eyes and looked carefully all around me, I could find delight, wonder, and beauty in a seemingly desolate, vacant place.

Psalm 121:1-2 (NIV) says: *I lift up my eyes to the mountains—where does my help come from? My help comes from the Lord, the Maker of heaven and earth.*

No matter how bleak the situation we are in, if we choose to look up, we can almost always find enough beauty and hope to see us through.

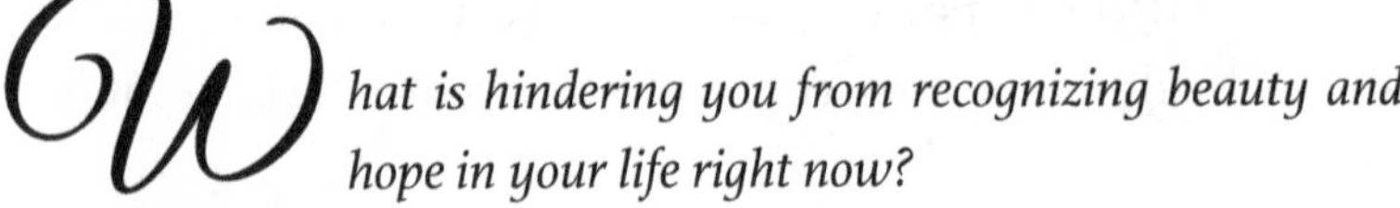

What is hindering you from recognizing beauty and hope in your life right now?

6

The Clash and Crash of Cultures

What if I don't rise from the bottom of the curve? In my first year in Afghanistan, I studied the graph depicting cultural adaptation patterns that we'd received during Pre-Field Orientation at the Oasis headquarters in June. *I am definitely over the honeymoon period of thinking everything different in Afghanistan is exotic or fun.*

"Looks like another sponge bath and dry shampoo," I mentioned to Michael as I left the upstairs apartment bathroom one morning. "Someone forgot to fill the roof water tank again, so a shower is out of the question." I threw my towel down on the bed and glared at him. What I wouldn't give for a wonderfully warm, powerful spray to start my day. Gravity water pressure was already sketchy unless the shower was on the ground floor and farther away from the tank.

"Sorry, hon. I will get Ali to run the pump right away. Maybe you can have a shower when you get home tonight?"

Much more tolerant of such inconveniences than me, my husband gave me a quick hug and hurried down the stairs. His workers were already waiting for him outside our door.

I did my best to freshen up, fix my hair, and squash my rising Eeyore attitude. What a way to start my workday. What could I wear to make myself happy?

With the hottest weather behind us, I enjoyed my Afghan outfits more. The long-sleeved tunics and full pants did not allow much air in to keep cool in full summer heat. However, they offered welcome coverage for cool temps and could be layered easily for the frigid days to come. I chose one of my favorite tailored ensembles in dark maroon, with stylish eyelet fabric on top and matching colored polyester pants with the typical elastic waist. Comfortable if not completely form flattering.

When inside the ISK compound walls, headscarves could be dropped to the shoulders but had to stay close at hand for trips out in public or for school visitors that needed special consideration not to offend. I collected a lovely array of scarves from local shop purchases and gifts from international friends and ISK families. I thought I was adjusting well to the clothing expectations and even found some DIY patterns back in the U.S. to sew long skirts and tunics using fabrics I found attractive.

But maybe not.

"You must not wear red so much. It is not for women, only small girls," my Dari teacher, Aqilla, told me one day in my office. She had a serious, concerned expression.

"Really?" I responded as I looked down at my ankle-length skirt with matching jacket, cut in a long conservative style. I selected this outfit specifically for wearing in Kabul. Yes, it was red, my favorite color, but nothing shiny or patterned, just solid red polyester. But crimson red, so apparently not subtle enough.

"I am sorry, but this color is not for respected women, certainly not for principals," she insisted in typical Afghan politeness. Her expression pleaded with me for understanding and agreement.

I sighed and sat back in my desk chair. I knew she had mustered extra courage to deliver this conversation, since I was her boss. In Afghanistan's indirect culture, she was breaking some taboos in her direct communication. But I trusted Aqilla to look out for me and ISK.

I'd hired her to teach Dari to our diverse student body and expatriate staff members. I spent more hours training and mentoring Aqilla than any other teacher at ISK. Although firmly ingrained in the Afghan educational pedagogy of drill and memorization, she tried to embrace modern interactive, student-centered instructional methods. We became close through all the time spent together at the school plus invitations to her home.

Now here she was looking out for my interest, saying what other Afghan women on the ISK campus were likely thinking, but would not speak to my face. I sadly put the offensive garment away and stuck to the browns, blacks, navies, and other subdued hues that Kabul women wore. But in a loving gesture, my new friend later surprised me with a Pashmina headscarf—soft, beautifully woven, and red.

The elastic waistbands and semi-fitted tunics came in handy for more than just comfort. I ended up gaining weight in my Kabul years. Not for lack of walking as I daily covered the full ISK complex to check with teachers and classrooms located in separate buildings along our street, each with multiple levels and stairs. We also had workout equipment in the common area of the Marble Mansion basement with various weight machine options, ellipticals, and treadmills, useful only when the electricity was on. I alternated floor exercises in my apartment with elliptical sessions on weeknights.

But it was the food that got me. Food that was generously supplied and easy to overindulge in. Not like my world back home where I carefully monitored all things food-wise for myself and my family.

"We need a chef," Byron said to me our first week in Kabul. "It will take too much time for teachers to shop in the bazaar since there is no all-inclusive grocery store. Then include the time they will have to spend cleaning everything with iodine to kill parasites, plus cooking time..." His science background came in handy to process the situation for the health of the team.

"How will we find someone who can cook for this many and understand English and Western tastes?" I questioned. "Where will we feed everyone? There are over twenty of us now."

He motioned me to follow him to the main floor of one of our staff buildings that housed single male teachers upstairs. "These walls can be opened to make a dining room and a serving window from the kitchen. We can make it work. We'll serve lunch to all staff Saturday through Thursday and only campus dwellers for dinner. Everyone can eat out or forage for themselves on Friday, the Holy Day, when the cook has the day off."

As we walked back to the admin building, Byron continued, "I'm checking with other international organizations in Kabul for a chef who would fit our needs. Since you have Home Economics training, you can work with him on menus.

And then you won't have to cook anymore." He winked at me in a friendly manner.

Byron had a great plan and God sent us the right man, Sakhi. He became very close to all of us, Western and Afghan alike, but particularly to Michael and me. He worked for ISK the entire time it was open, almost ten years. He could have worked most anywhere with his culinary training, wonderful attitude, and work ethic.

"What are you doing, Sakhi?" I walked in one afternoon and surveyed the kitchen now outfitted with an institutional stove and oven, plus a large quantity of cooking pans. I knew the menu that night was to be hamburgers and fries, but nothing in his preparation setup looked familiar. "What are you dropping into that pot of hot oil?" I watched as he reached for another circle of raw ground beef from the large tray beside the stove.

With his trademark smile that caused his eyes to disappear in his jolly face, Sakhi said, "I am cooking the beef burgers. Why you ask me? You make the menu." He held the patty in mid-air, looking at me intently.

"No, no, stop, we don't deep fry hamburgers. They will be dry and tough." I turned off the pot of oil and held the tray for him to return the lucky beef saved from overcooked death. "With so many burgers to make, I suggest you broil a full tray in the oven for a short time, flipping them only once. Let me show you."

He watched and listened carefully, making Dari notes in his ever-present notebook, full of recipes and other information he needed for shopping and preparing so many unfamiliar dishes. Weekly, he made traditional Afghan dishes for us too, which most of the team totally enjoyed. His humor and positive outlook kept us well emotionally while his careful food preparation helped us stay well physically.

"Oh, Sakhi, good job! Where did you find the celery?" I grabbed a handful of cut pieces off the buffet line for my lunch one day.

"My friend call me early in morning while on my way to bazaar for shopping. I always look for broccoli and celery that you put on list, but not find it. Today, yes." Sakhi added more celery to the pile as teachers crowded around for the rare treat, loading peanut butter, raisins, or Ranch dressing on the crunchy stalks. Sakhi watched with interest at these condiment choices and relished in the obvious delight of those he served.

"Do you like it?" I asked him. "Do you eat celery?"

With a twinkle in his eye, he said, "No, I no like celery. I like *salary*!"

My full-out laughter joined with his customary snickering giggle and caught the attention of the dining hall patrons. Sakhi's advanced English pun was repeated time and time again with great admiration and affection for our dear friend and chef.

General living requirements hit a comfortable rhythm for me with ISK's unique blend of Central Asian and Western preferences. But I was accustomed to certain things working efficiently in the modern, tech-savvy world. And I needed them in order to operate a top-tier school every day, especially electricity and Internet access and speed.

"What just happened?" I looked at my IT staff member in panic as I watched the monitor screens go blank one evening in the computer lab. All the Afghan heads popped up from their keyboard tapping and began calling out for help. We were about two hours into the four-hour TOEFL iBT exam with about a dozen test-takers hard at work.

"I don't know. I think the electricity went off," my coworker quietly replied as he jumped from his control desk to check outside the classroom. His grimace matched the sinking feeling I was experiencing.

From the first day we arrived in Kabul and began setting up ISK and staff housing, internet connectivity and power outages challenged our microwave Westerner patience. Michael learned more than he ever wanted to know about generators and concrete-building-wiring issues in his early weeks of campus maintenance. Kabul city power was increasing all the time and lowering our outrageous diesel fuel costs, but it was not consistent in strength or length of operation. It was one thing to have my DVD viewing interrupted, knowing I could finish watching another time, or wait a day to send emails back to the States. But this particular electricity failure was disastrous.

My IT guy returned with a frustrated expression. "Ali switched us from generator to city power like he usually does when it comes on. He didn't realize we would lose all the TOEFL test downloads on the computers. It was an honest mistake, really." He lifted his hands in surrender to the problem that could not be fixed today.

"This is awful." I looked around the room at the testing participants, some seniors at ISK trying to get a good score for college applications, some businessmen from faraway cities trying to qualify for jobs overseas. They had each paid $190 for this important assessment.

I had worked hard to get approval as an official TOEFL, SAT, and ACT testing site in Afghanistan to serve our college-bound students fully. I'd hoped we could also serve ambitious

Afghan adults who needed to prove English proficiency to achieve their goals for higher education outside the country or international employment.

"We will not be able to finish the test today. I am so sorry," I explained to the angry faces staring at me. "We will find out what can be done to give you another test opportunity as soon as possible without additional payment."

The testers left, speaking to one another in Dari, leaving me to wonder what they were saying. I guessed it wasn't anything positive about ISK. But the real culprit of the disaster was the elusive electricity beyond our control.

The culture shock reverse bell-curve forecasted a trouble spot at about four to six months into a first-year experience. Here the newbie in a strange environment might struggle with anger and mockery. Meaning constant exposure to different, unfamiliar traditions or behaviors can elicit negative judgments like *that's so stupid* or *that's ridiculous.* Eventually, the goal is to pull upward and learn to tolerate, understand, and move to a peaceful acceptance of the new place.

I found my own journey fairly true to the predicted pattern. Eventually, I found ways to make my expectations for daily life realistic and have a *plan B* ready for particularly important needs (like emailing in accreditation paperwork or graduate school assignments days early in case the internet went down.) But one pervasive cultural clash never became acceptable to me, or any ISK female.

The general Afghan message concerning the low worth of women was intolerable. The culture practically denied them any possible contribution to society beyond producing offspring. Western women and most of our enlightened male counterparts rejected this belief strongly.

For me, growing up in the American '70s era of equality

demonstrations for race as well as gender, the Afghan female discrimination was a maddening step back in time. I enjoyed unlimited freedom and opportunity growing up compared to the girls and women of past and present Afghanistan. During my college years, I even completed an internship in Washington, D.C., dedicated to leadership development and career preparation for young women.

I also attended such gatherings as the 1976 Hemispheric Conference for Women in Miami. Enlightened and empowered female leaders from North and South America demanded strong mandates for solving health issues, childcare concerns, and workforce inequality. I soaked in the feminist agenda to increase recognition of the value of women for the betterment of themselves and their society. In true solidarity, I owned a copy of Helen Reddy's album, "I Am Woman."

But in my seven years in Kabul, I never drove myself anywhere. I never walked alone on a public street. I submitted to the full coverage dress code for women, no matter the weather or discomfort. I endured the ominous, anonymous male stares in the marketplace and even in the Afghan government buildings while conducting ISK business. I had men and ISK fathers speak to me in condescending tones and dismiss my authority when I did not accommodate their demands. Teen boys on bicycles enjoyed harassing us when walking on the street, trying to push us into the ditch. It was not *every* man's attitude toward women in Afghanistan, but it was far too common. I didn't realize how much it would influence me over time.

I probably can't do that...

When I first heard that thought pop into my mind while thinking through a problem, I stopped in my tracks. Like an invisible gas seeping into a room undetected until the occupants fell over in critical condition, I felt the cultural message that females were weak, dumb, and *so much less than men* working its way into my confidence core.

No, not true! I know better. I will not let these present lifestyle reductions and cultural restrictions re-identify and dictate who I am as a woman. Especially since I know what God says about His love and appreciation for women as well as men. Jesus taught and modeled equal sacrifice and equal eternal rewards for both genders.

I, along with my female teammates and international friends, committed to pushing back these vaporous cultural lies and being a beacon of hope to the Afghan women we served. If this resulted in my remaining in the low dip of the cultural adaptation curve, then so be it. I would rather crash and clash with this cultural difference than believe it was right, better, or in any way true for women to be invisible, unimportant, enslaved, or harshly treated.

And there was no better way to fight a long-standing cultural belief than education. At ISK, we encouraged our brave female students in every way we could to dream and have confidence in their abilities. We wanted our young men to receive the counter-cultural message that they needed women to help lift society and make the world better for everyone. We did this intentionally—but hopefully also naturally—through our respectful treatment of one another as men and women, coworkers, bosses, employees, and married couples.

I don't know if we won any converts to our equal-treatment mantra at ISK from the traditional Afghan families and their male students. After all, their own sisters rarely attended anything but the free government girls' schools, certainly not a tuition-required, co-ed school run by foreigners. We gave it our best effort and perhaps slowly, this counter-cultural message will rise from the bottom of the curve for Afghans and become accepted as human rights for all.

The Unveiled Truth: I knew that my cross-cultural adaptation would be challenging, like any transition in life, but I hoped it would be rewarding.

When we are learning new ways to do things, we need to remember different is not always bad or wrong, just different.

If you are willing, you can pull out of the foggy, frustrating stage of transition, like the bottom of the culture shock curve, and come to appreciate, if not prefer, your new situation. Being willing to adapt opens you up to relate and connect to more people in this big, diverse world.

Where in your life are you embracing the challenge of adapting?

7

Only the Strong Survive

On Michael's first trip to Afghanistan in 2002, he and a long-time friend watched some Afghan men smoothing watered-down cement over a broken, bullet-pocked wall with nothing more than hand tools.

"Give me an Afghan worker over a former communist any day," Our friend commented. He had been a global worker for almost a decade with non-governmental organizations in a former Soviet state. "From what I've observed in my time in Kabul, Afghans take initiative. They get up every morning and get it done."

He and Michael started back for their guest house. "The people in Uzbekistan are afraid to think or act for themselves after always being told what to do. Gotta respect the Afghan survival attitude or instinct, whichever it is."

I remembered this story from Michael's trip as I stood watching our Afghan staff renovate the ISK campus. Our friend's observations proved to be a true assessment of the varied tribes and people groups that lived within Afghanistan. The years of devastation pressed them to live for the day and not put too much expectation on tomorrow. I wondered about their hopes and vision for the future, but I decided I needed to connect with them in the present. Though I struggled to attach myself to Kabul, I knew there were valuable lessons I could learn from its people.

I may have been the one dragged to a war-torn country nearly against my will, but it wasn't just me who wished things were different. Not only have Afghans endured over forty years of war and constant change of national leadership, but they have suffered through years of drought and all the hardship that goes with extremely diminished natural resources. The average life expectancy for men and women hovers in the forties, and children die too often in pregnancy, birth, and the fragile years before age five. Afghans display both a resignation and resiliency about life. They accept they cannot count on the future, so they maximize the opportunities each day presents.

I found myself in awe of how Afghans mustered the will to overcome hardship and not turn into stony, unfeeling human beings. Some of the testimonies from my national staff and ISK families left me shaking my head.

"How long did your family live in Iran?" I asked Noorullah, one of our national staff, as he hammered into my office's concrete-brick wall to hang my framed diplomas. Such credentials are highly respected in Afghanistan, so I'd been advised to bring them overseas with me.

He stopped to look at me before hammering in the next nail. "We were refugees there many years. My father set up a computer center with all his saved money. We went to school and worked there to help him. It was good. But then Iran government said Afghans were too much trouble, a drain on the country, and made us return. We lost our business, everything. Now we start over." He went back to his task without more details or signs of anger. He'd just told it the way it was.

I returned to my computer, not completely focused on the emails loading in, thinking instead how I had more in common with displaced Afghans than I would have thought.

Like Noorullah, I needed to gather inner strength for my rebooted life in this strange land if I was to thrive.

As the principal of ISK, I received invitations to birthday celebrations, family dinners, and all-day weddings. In the bazaar streets, I may have felt overlooked and treated as invisible, but not in an Afghan home. I was treated like a queen. This presented more opportunities to listen and learn from Afghans outside the comfy, Western bubble I had enjoyed. I did not always feel like heading out to another engagement where I needed to be *on*. Slippers and hot tea in the privacy of my apartment called to me after a full work week, but I rarely declined an invite.

"C'mon, it'll be great food and a chance to get off campus." Michael read the email invitation from the Daudzai family. "You really like their children, and Mr. Daudzai is a remarkable cabinet leader for President Karzai." He looked at me with a winsome smile.

"I know, it's just I'm exhausted, and it'll be late when we finally get home. You know the evening won't be short with all the dinner courses." I sighed and went into the bathroom to wash my face and reapply my make-up. Mrs. Daudzai would be dressed well, so I needed to remain professional looking.

Often, several of the school staff would be invited as a group to these family dinners, up to as many as fifteen to twenty of us on occasion. Michael enjoyed these social interactions even more than I. We would be ushered into the salon of the home, a large multi-purpose room, where we attempted to fold up stiff American legs on the floor toshaks provided as a seat and backrest. Some owned Western chairs and sofas which we appreciated.

"How do you like Afghanistan?" Mr. Daudzai began. The home was lovely and spacious enough to accommodate a large dinner party. Often big screen TVs would be playing in the background so Mr. Daudzai could keep abreast of national and international news, but never so much he slighted his guests.

"We are glad to be here. I find Afghan people so friendly and only wish I knew more Dari," Michael responded as he took a chair near our host, often sitting on the other side of Khalid who was a regular guest along with Byron and me.

With excellent English skills, I marveled at Mr. Daudzai's ability to communicate with us about most any topic. When answering questions about Afghanistan, he expressed realism and optimism at the same time—amazing. We never tried to press him for confidential information, just insights into the future of the country's stability, since ISK was contingent on such to remain in the country. He appeared to enjoy the bantering back and forth with educated foreigners and made us feel welcomed into his family.

I smiled politely and let the men chat for a minute, watching Mrs. Daudzai and her daughters set out dried fruits, nuts, candy, and tea for all of us. The women rarely sat with the guests.

"So, Marzia, can I help your mom with anything?" I asked my ISK student. I was well aware of the effort her mother was going through to host a room full of people.

"Oh, no, Mrs. Goolsby, she would not allow that! My sisters and I will help. Please just have some tea and sweets." I thanked her and continued to watch as the teen girls followed their mother's directions. The younger brothers disappeared to play video games after politely greeting the guests.

It took some time for me to embrace my station as a guest, feeling disconnected from the hostess. Mrs. Daudzai did not speak English but would join the table after she served the entrees, having one of her children translate for her to converse with me or other female teachers at the table. If the hostess was more traditional, she would not sit with her guests at all, leaving me to engage in casual conversation with the father, students, and other ISK team members present.

After dinner, when we retired to the salon with more tea and fresh fruit, I often showed my hostess and ISK students family pictures from a pocket-size album. "This is my first granddaughter, Cora, and that is her mother, my daughter Sarah, and her husband. Here is my other daughter Anna and my son, John, who is a musician."

I watched as Mrs. Daudzai looked at the photos while her daughter translated my comments in Dari. She smiled and spoke to her daughter as she passed the album back to me.

"My mother says you look very young to have grandchildren, Mrs. Goolsby. And where is your son's wife?" I shook my head, not bothering to explain why my son was still a bachelor. Unmarried sons were unheard of in the Afghan culture.

Rejoining the large group conversation, I asked Mr. Daudzai in which part of Afghanistan their ancestral home was located and where they had lived besides Kabul.

"My work for President Karzai has taken us to Iran and Pakistan in diplomatic service. Then he requested I return to Afghanistan to serve as his Chief of Staff. I was honored to do so. But this has been difficult for my family with so many relocations." Mr. Daudzai looked thoughtfully at his wife and children, who gazed back with love and respect.

Our hosts shared their experiences with other foreigners in the other places they'd lived. These stories often included humorous anecdotes of cultural learning and mistakes made.

I tried to offer interesting, entertaining, translatable stories of my family to make a connection as well.

As we shared our lives, we found common ground despite how different our lives had been and still were. All of us desired a peaceful place to raise our families, to be able to provide financially for our needs, and to get our children educated.

I always brought our hosts a gift of candy or fruit to show good manners and gratitude, but I soon recognized I received more than I gave. I was offered a transparent view into their challenging lives. I gained respect for the resiliency and commitment of our ISK families who worked toward better times for their country and the world around them. Their investment in their children and careers demonstrated their deep belief that no matter the bleakness of present-day Afghanistan, new leaders with education and informed perspectives could make a difference in the future of their homeland.

That was the reason I'd come to Kabul, to make a difference through shaping young minds. Evenings with families like the Daudzais inspired and motivated me to continue, no matter how exhausting and sometimes futile my efforts felt.

However, not all parents had the resources to pay for ISK's top-tier education or even meet the daily needs of their families. Children are a prize for Afghans—especially for those who worked in the village fields or owned businesses and needed the extra hands. But many children presented a problem as well—more mouths to feed created many challenges for the war-stricken natives. And when multiple, closely-timed births occurred, medical issues could become overwhelming.

"I need to bring Marafat to the campus," Sharon, a senior staff member's wife, delivered this news to me one spring day in my office. She held a tiny baby girl she'd brought over from the nearby hospital. "She won't interfere with the school. I'll keep her at our apartment."

Sharon often volunteered each week with the newborns at the hospital, especially the special needs infants. She also taught classes in the community about prenatal health and safe childbirth. "This little one was only a couple of pounds at birth and needs to be fed small amounts of formula around the clock. The nurses in the hospital will not take on the time-consuming care for such a weak baby. Can I ask any willing teachers to help me with her in their off-time?

"Where is her mother?" I came from around my desk to peer at the delicate bundle, too weak to make any sounds. I touched the miniature hand and stroked her soft, dark hair.

So tiny, so vulnerable. Do we need one more Afghan child dependent on our team? Do I need one more thing to feel responsible for?

"She had to return to her village with her husband. They have no family in Kabul to stay with. This was her first live birth after eleven pregnancies. I bet she isn't even mid-twenties yet."

We exchanged tight looks of frustration and pain for this young woman and her inescapable life situation. The new mother was living with a domineering mother-in-law and her husband's other wife had borne many children, likely making her feel worthless. We had heard such stories before, especially among the uneducated populace. They were ruled by tradition, not reason or medical research.

"Absolutely, check around. I'm sure you can find many willing ladies to help nurture this little one. Let me know if you need anything more from me." I turned to gaze out my office window as my teammate with the pink bundle left to enlist her army of nursemaids.

I hope I'm doing the right thing. Running the school is difficult enough without this heart-capturing drama in our midst. Will one more Afghan child be a good thing for this under-resourced family? But the poor mother, so many lost babies! How can I interfere with helping her little miraculous survivor? Please, God, don't let this baby die while in our team's care.

We all celebrated when Marafat grew to a robust five pounds by the time we left for summer break in early June. When I returned in August, I found out her family had retrieved her in late June, but a month later, our little ISK wonder baby had died.

"What? How did this happen? She was doing so well." I sat with Sharon in the campus dining hall and stopped the sob welling up in my throat. My worst fear had come true, Marafat had not survived. Even if she hadn't died while under our care, I felt the loss just as much as if she had. I didn't relish the job my teammate had in reporting the bad news to the other ladies who had fed, rocked, hugged, and prayed for this precious baby.

Maybe we shouldn't have gotten involved? But how would we have felt if we hadn't tried? No, I physically shook my head in response to my internal debate.

As if knowing my thoughts, Sharon continued, "We cannot predict the future, right? We did as God asked us and surely the love she received here was a great gift. Sadly, the family had no money for formula, and the other wife refused to nurse the baby along with her own infant. Marafat got dysentery, probably from unboiled water in her bottles of tea, and got dehydrated from the constant diarrhea. She wasn't strong enough to handle it."

We sipped our cups of tea in silence. So pointless. So curable in most situations, but not in distant, poor villages. Tears escaped my eyes.

Still, large families are absolutely the norm, especially for those Afghan men who exercised their right to have multiple wives. The Muslim culture permits up to four wives. Not many families followed this tradition at ISK, but some did.

Another cultural practice we found difficult to embrace was first-cousin marriages, knowing the impact on children's health and possible birth complications. Families trust unions with extended relatives over outsiders. Children with special needs have little hope in Afghanistan due to the lack of social, medical, or educational resources taken for granted in the West. These hidden family members see little outside the walls of their home compound.

"Please, miss, you have my other children enrolled at ISK. One more should not be a problem." The wealthy father sat across from my desk with an unfamiliar wife and an elementary child who appeared to have severe cerebral palsy. We did teach several of the man's sons—never his daughters—from two other wives. "There is no school for him in Kabul. I will pay additional fees. Please."

With a pain in my heart and stomach, I took a deep breath and delivered my verdict.

"It is not possible. I am sorry." I used my go-to phrase *not possible*, having learned early that *no* just invited continued pleas in this culture. "I wish we could help, but my teachers do not have the resources to help students needing separate, special attention. They have to work hard with their full classrooms of students still learning English. All our buildings have stairs, and we could not make a wheelchair work. I am sorry." I glanced again at the innocent child with no educational options.

Being principal was hard.

I have a strong side and a soft side. But being principal in a patriarchal culture with a majority of male students, my tough side came out more than I would have preferred.

"If it hadn't been you fulfilling that role, it would have to be someone just like you." One of my very best educator friends and mentor spoke these words to me in response to my worries about having to be so often hard-nosed in my job.

I knew she was right. I learned from the Afghans all around me about what is needed to survive in tough places and tough life situations. Strength was needed, yes, but I also needed to embrace all types of emotions, rather than try to avoid or escape them. I had to press through the pain to arrive at the victories.

Pain and struggle, achievement and joy; each has its necessary place in the classroom of lifelong learning.

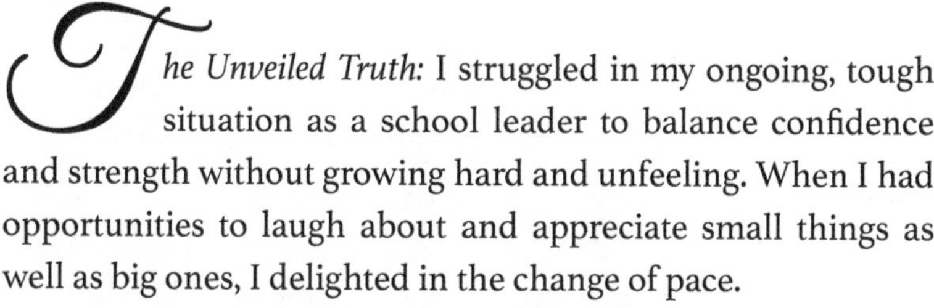

The Unveiled Truth: I struggled in my ongoing, tough situation as a school leader to balance confidence and strength without growing hard and unfeeling. When I had opportunities to laugh about and appreciate small things as well as big ones, I delighted in the change of pace.

Part of thriving and not just surviving through hard times

is embracing the full gamut of emotions we are created to feel, not just showcasing strength nonstop. We are not machines, after all.

Make intentional efforts to engage in your preferred relaxed activities. When possible, let others carry the ball of responsibility. Practice self-care. Be aware of the mounting toll of your outgoing energy and ascribe to healthy boundaries.

What symptoms are you currently experiencing that signal a lack of healthy life balance and what changes can you make?

8

For the Good of Girls

"Look at those skipping schoolgirls! What a precious picture of happiness and freedom," I mentioned to Karen as we walked outside the ISK barriers with a male guard. It was our turn to pick up some chocolate croissants at the nearby Afghan *French Bakery* to share with admin staff for an end-of-the-week treat. The swarm of young females bouncing down the street to their public schoolyard was a favorite sight.

"It's unfair that the boys can wear whatever they want," Karen remarked. "Why must the girls dress in black pantsuits and white headscarves? Good grief. Such a double standard." Suddenly she chuckled and discreetly pointed. "That pair is pushing for individual expression. You go, girls!"

I followed her gesture to see two of the smaller girls with Barbie backpacks, light-up athletic shoes, and pink ball caps perched on top of their mandatory headscarves. They held hands and chatted head-to-head as they made their way to school. Karen and I exchanged smiles in celebration of these spunky gals.

During the Russian rule in the early 80s, education was readily available to both genders and no *chadari*, another word for *burkah*, in sight. Men and women attended school together from primary through university.

Once the nation went under Taliban rule, only boys were permitted to attend. Quite the setback.

When enrolling his two oldest girls at ISK, one father detailed to me the deeply secretive, illegal plan he'd concocted under Taliban rule to help his daughters. "Back then, our family joined others to make sure our four daughters received education. We filled one house salon with sewing machines, one for each girl. If any unknown visitor entered the schoolroom, machines appeared, and students picked up garments to sew. Then the students returned to reading and writing when the all-clear signal sounded."

I was impressed by his courage and commitment to education under such strict penalties as imprisonment for such activities.

Following the fall of the Taliban, free government schools opened to girls. But problems continued to make access for females limited. Approximately thirty percent of Afghan teachers are women, with a higher percentage in the urban areas. Traditional families will not send their daughters to a university for teacher training or jobs in remote areas of the country without a *male* family member chaperone. Conservative families refuse to send their daughters to school where there are no female teachers. Girls' classes have to be held at separate times or in separate buildings from their male counterparts. Kabul facilities were sorely limited in the early 2000s, and today they are not much better.

Things are even worse for village girls wanting to learn.

"Come to the Wardak province with us. I want you to see some champions for educating girls outside of Kabul." An American friend, who led a non-governmental organization (NGO) in Afghanistan, proffered the invitation to Michael and me in our first year at ISK. "We will leave early in the morning and be back the same day."

Byron was not keen on me venturing so far from ISK security. He determined Khalid should accompany us, which he was delighted to do as this was a beautiful area of Afghanistan with apple orchards and farmland.

"Michael and Khalid, you bring her back. She's the only principal we've got." Byron stood with his hands on his hips and a non-smiling expression as we got into a car with our vetted driver outside the admin building.

We traveled the early morning hours outside of Kabul on rough, unpaved dusty roads. Khalid recounted tales of relocating to Wardak from Kabul for a week of wartime reprieve during *rocket rain* between the Afghan warlords.

"Who is that man by the side of the road up ahead?" I scooted forward to look out the window where a tall, turbaned figure had suddenly appeared though we'd not seen towns, buildings, or people for miles. "Where did he come from?" Then I noticed the familiar strap across his shoulders like those our security guards wore while patrolling ISK campus and around Kabul. He was carrying a weapon under his cloak.

"He is a village leader." Our NGO friend said from his spot in the front seat. "We are picking him up to take us into the heart of Wardak province. He will be our bodyguard in case we run into any trouble." Our friend hadn't turned around, so he missed our backseat, wide-eyed reaction.

We need a bodyguard? Maybe Byron was right. I shouldn't be here. Michael squeezed my hand under my long scarf but did not look at me. I said nothing, feeling frozen in the moment like a movie scene.

When we stopped near the stranger, Khalid got out of the front seat to join us in the back. We moved over to make room for our lanky young friend. I met Khalid's eyes and he gave me a thumbs up, instinctively knowing my concern. He was well acquainted with such arrangements, having grown up under the Taliban rule. Guns did not have the same effect on him, being a child of wartime, as they did on me.

Our new rider folded up his long legs and squeezed into the front seat. He laid his AK-47 across his lap. Greetings were exchanged in Pashto among the men, the other national language besides Dari, belonging exclusively to the Pashtun tribe. The word Pashtun is synonymous with Afghan and this people group forms the majority tribe in the country. Wardak is largely a Pashtun province with a strong Taliban presence, although Tajiks and Hazaras also live there.

Our newest rider kept his gaze straight ahead, only exchanging brief Pashto whispers to our driver to direct his road choices. He did not engage with the rest of us, as if we weren't there. It was weird but not too alarming.

"This family we are going to visit has made incredible personal sacrifices to help girls have educational opportunities." Our friend turned to address us once the car had started down the dusty, pitted road again. "The three schools we will visit are all gifts from this wealthy farmer and his family."

Within thirty minutes, we came upon a large compound with cows, sheep, chickens, and haystacks gathered in the center of three buildings. I happily climbed out of the back after two hours of crowded, bumpy travel and stretched my stiff limbs.

I followed our NGO friend and Khalid and looked behind me for the rest of our travel companions. Michael was coming along, but the driver stayed with the car.

Our silent bodyguard slipped out of sight as mysteriously as he had appeared.

We entered the family home, and even though it was only mid-morning, a full meal awaited us. Michael exchanged respectful bows and handshakes with the men. I smiled and nodded and sat in the place the mother indicated for us on the toshaks around the salon walls. The customary vinyl tablecloth had been spread over the middle of the floor in front of us and the daughters brought in the food.

"I just had breakfast," I whispered to Khalid who clapped his hands at the full platters of rice, native Wardak apples, dried apricots, and tender mutton.

"I can always eat such wonderful food. Just like my grandmother makes." Khalid proceeded to consume enough for three people, to the obvious delight of the mother and daughters who'd prepared the feast. When I had Khalid translate my admiration of the stack of fresh, shiny, red apples before me, I was rewarded with a bag full to take home. The perfect gift for a teacher.

After the meal, we followed our farmer benefactor to the first girls' school, right on his home compound in a large open room with no windows, mud-covered walls, and a dirt floor. Michael, Khalid, and our NGO friend stayed close to the door to avoid offending the female occupants who are not supposed to be viewed by male outsiders. I followed my guide inside, and although male, he was well-known and therefore allowed to come to the front of the classroom where the teacher stood waiting for us.

"Hello! Good morning!" The young teacher spoke to me and we exchanged cheek kisses.

She looked like a teenager, but her cheerful expression exuded confidence in her role.

"Good morning. Thank you for allowing me to come." I turned to view the students. The age span looked to be six to sixteen, perhaps with forty or more girls sitting on the dirt floor, with the smallest ones up front. Instead of black-white uniforms, the group wore a bright array of colored headscarves and well-worn tunic pantsuits. The eager faces stared intently at me. As a principal—a highly respected position, even for a woman, especially a foreign woman—I was treated like a celebrity.

"A cup. A cat. An apple." The girls stood for me and recited the list from a broken whiteboard on one wall using their newly acquired English skills. They performed an English song that had more unified diction than tune but clearly well-rehearsed. I asked Khalid to translate my words of praise for their miniature recital.

I was flooded by the girls when leaving and willingly hugged and exchanged cheek kisses as much as possible. Signs of poverty were evident, but the female students were clearly happy to be in school. I felt connected to each of the simple, courageous Wardak schools we visited as they endeavored to provide a brighter future to the women of their community.

Years later, back in the States, whenever I give presentations about these local schools and show the pictures of those precious faces, tears come to my eyes. Some of those schools closed after our visit, or rather, disappeared because of nighttime mortar blasts thanks to backward, incomprehensible Taliban actions. Unbelievable. Outrageous. Upsetting.

But don't think that the country villagers were the only ones facing the hardships of out-dated thinking. Our own Afghan ISK families had to actively rebel against numerous cultural mores and endure extended family members' judgment to make sure their sons and daughters received a top-level academic education. For many in the country, ISK was a frowned-upon, co-ed school with foreign teachers and a secular curriculum. However, neither the national Afghan schools nor the newer Afghan private schools could deliver such a quality education due to many circumstances beyond their control. The parents who paid for the privilege of attending ISK—when the government schools offered free education—deserved a medal, in my opinion.

"Here is one of my favorite fathers," I mentioned to a teacher on morning car duty as a white SUV pulled up to the ISK entrance. "Watch him."

The Afghan man got out of his expensive chauffeured car to personally hand each of his three daughters and one son their backpacks and kiss them on the forehead as they entered the schoolyard.

"Clearly, he loves and values his daughters as much as his son. Glad he returned from Canada to serve in the government. Afghanistan needs men like him." I turned back to my office, renewed again in our mission to educate and change the future of this land.

We had many government leaders' children at ISK, who desired quality education and also needed the high-level security we offered. A particular group drawn to us were female Members of Parliament (MP). In the 2010 elections, sixty-nine women won hard-fought odds to take seats in the 249-member parliament. Male MPs interrupted, ignored, laughed at, snored at, and even threatened the women for speaking up and basically doing their job. Often the women's own relatives pressed the hardest for them to vote in agreement with the male leaders and not bring perceived shame upon the family.

"You are saying you would sacrifice your own three daughters for the sake of all the women in Afghanistan?" I questioned the lovely female MP sitting across the desk in my office at ISK.

"Yes, it is a sacrifice that someday I hope they understand," she responded in perfect English, learned during her Western education and years of living abroad. I sighed and never took my eyes off her perfect, cosmetic-covered face, frozen in a polite, unreadable expression. We had been debating for several minutes (and on several other occasions) about the troublesome behavior of her boy-crazy, flirtatious, non-academic junior high daughter and the low performance of her two elementary girls.

"Your daughters all have low grades, and since English is not their problem, unlike most of the struggling students, I think you should share with them how important education is and motivate them to do better. Spend time reading together and review their homework." I spread the girls' recent report cards on my desk in front of the mother. "I was a working mother, too. It's hard to balance work and family needs, but it can be done."

She politely glanced at the documents and nodded but made no commitment as she shook my hand and left with her entourage of guards and driver. From my American viewpoint, the mother was too busy serving the millions of Afghan women to personally oversee the needs of her own little women at home. She frustrated me with her seemingly easy release of responsibility for her children to others. Sometimes being a principal is more about educating parents than their children, but also recognizing my own biases.

One widowed Afghan woman returned from the U.S. to serve in Parliament with her youngest daughter, Sheena, an American born and bred girl. The daughter had no desire to live in un-fun, boring Afghanistan. She entered fifth grade at ISK and quickly became a regular visitor to the principal's office.

"Why did you have a knife in your lunch box, Sheena? You know they are not allowed at school." I tried to get the pre-teen to look at me, but she kept her eyes downcast and just shrugged her shoulders. "You pointed it at Hamid and acted like you were going to hurt him. What is going on between you two?" I waited.

Silence.

"Look, Sheena, I know you're unhappy and lonely with only you and your mom in Kabul. I know you left your friends and older sisters behind in Virginia. I want to help you, and so does your teacher. But you must stop taking people's things, lying to your mom, and telling wild stories to get attention." I moved to sit beside the sad girl and put my arm around her.

Finally, Sheena spoke in apathetic tones, still not meeting my gaze but leaning into me. "There is nothing to do here. I hate Kabul and want to go home. Maybe if I flunk out, my mom will send me back to America." I felt her tears on my shoulder and stroked her hair in sympathy.

The staff at ISK understood the struggles of our transplanted American-Afghan students, particularly the girls. Sheena no longer lived in a world of freedom that offered her daily choices of fast food, modern fashions, social engagements, and media entertainment. Instead, she encountered

Afghanistan's reduced resources, such as no malls or parks or theaters to hang out with friends, and a walled home environment with constant restrictions.

Sheena was like many Western-raised children who returned with their Afghan parents to rebuild the needy nation with their bilingual skills and dual-cultural understanding. The parents had great job opportunities, but the students were thrust into a foreign, depressing lifestyle.

Second to the culture shock, her large, anonymous U.S. public-school experience had been traded for a small, everyone-knows-your-business private school environment. Soon enough, the students came to appreciate the personal attention with smaller classes and better teacher-student ratios, but at first, they felt exposed and defensive. Sheena was not used to so much scrutiny for all her antics and low performance.

"Let's go visit Miss Crump in the library." I gave her a tissue to wipe her face and stood up. "She has offered to help you with your missing homework assignments after school today. Things will get better, but you need to do your part, Sheena."

I escorted her from my office down the hall to the library and exchanged knowing looks over the girl's head with Miss Crump. We both knew one-on-one attention, as well as tutoring, would help with Sheena's grades and emotional needs. I became an extension to Sheena's family, along with her teachers and other ISK staff. Her mother frequently showered us with gifts of jewelry and clothing to show her gratitude.

One day, Sheena's mother came to my office with a strained face and puffy eyes. Her bodyguard waited outside my doorway. *What has Sheena done now?*

"Oh, Mrs. Goolsby, I am so worried. I have not slept in two days. ISK might be shut down or attacked by the Taliban and then what will I do with my daughter?" The mother dabbed at her eyes with her headscarf.

"What's happened?" I stood to lead her to a chair and sat beside her, anxiety creeping in.

But it was not Sheena this time, instead, it was one of her classmates.

As Sheena's mother unveiled the details about secret, romantic meetings happening on our campus between Sheena's Pakistani friend and an older Afghan male student, I joined her shocked and worried state. If these youthful, sensual encounters proved true, ISK could be in danger. Western mores would not judge a young couple so harshly, but in the Islamic Republic of Afghanistan—oh, yes! We would be in big trouble.

"I will talk to Dr. Greene right away. Thank you for coming to me. Please tell Sheena not to say anything to her classmates or anyone. Will you do that?" She nodded and we hugged for a few minutes before I gave her back to her guard and headed for my boss's office.

"Come in," Byron called as I knocked on his door. When I walked in and sat across from his desk, he looked at my expression and stopped his two-finger typing immediately. "What's up? You look really upset."

After only a few minutes of conversation, Byron called in back up from other senior admin staff members. We formulated a plan to get the facts, starting with the seventeen-year-old young man. He denied any part in the crime, even swearing on his mother's name. We interviewed more students until we felt confident we had the full story.

Lastly, I brought the fourteen-year-old girl in for questioning. With little provocation, she confessed everything. "We love each other. He wants to marry me." She sobbed.

I closed my eyes in disbelief at those naïve words. *She watches too many romantic movies. She has no idea what is happening.*

Romantic movies turned out to be part of the problem, combined with losing her father at a young age. Her European stepfather had no experience raising children, particularly a teenage girl trying to make sense of life in an ultra-conservative Muslim culture. She enjoyed reading mature romantic novels and feasting her eyes on PG-13, or even R-rated films that they watched as a family.

"I thought since we watched the videos together at home it would be okay. I am so sorry." The mother and stepfather realized their mistake when everything came to light. The girl's older Pakistani brother told me he had tried to alert their parents of the danger and inappropriateness of her pastime activities, but they hadn't listened to his advice.

This sad story of immature, unwise, red-blooded youths ended like a modern-day *Romeo and Juliet*. ISK immediately expelled the young man permanently. The shamed boy's relatives sent him quickly to another country, mainly for protection against extended relatives' repercussions, perhaps never to return to Afghanistan. Even in the face of true repentance, we could not allow the girl to continue on campus at ISK either. We needed to publicly show our intolerance for inappropriate male-female behavior at our already controversial American school.

"We are very grateful, Mrs. Goolsby, for all you have done for our family." The young lady's parents came with flowers and sweets to Karen's desk in the admin building. "Please thank the teachers also for sending assignments and allowing our daughter to finish the semester at home. We are moving to the Netherlands this summer and hope to start over where this problem is not known by everyone."

I shook hands with the parents and hugged the girl goodbye as they gathered their paperwork to leave ISK and transfer to a new school in the fall.

"Thank you, Mrs. Goolsby." Sheena and her MP mother came by my office after the clouds of tension cleared. "Absolutely, you saved the school."

While appreciating their gratitude, my heart felt torn. I hated to see such a harsh ending to normal growing-up experimentation by our Romeo and Juliet, but these were not normal times or circumstances for ISK students or staff. Hard decisions had to be made to protect the fragile acceptance ISK presently enjoyed. All eyes, some friendly, some adversarial, watched our every move. While feeling like the cost to sacrifice this naïve girl and foolish, arrogant young man was high, we had to consider the bigger picture for ISK to continue.

I happened to run into the young lady's stepfather at a restaurant a year later as he returned to work occasionally in Kabul. He came over to our table as Michael and I enjoyed a brief time away from campus and updated me on his family. Our *ISK Juliet* had made the most of her forced transition by making new friends and developing a new self-respect. She was thriving in a new place, freely exploring all it means to be a young, capable woman. He thanked me again with emotion for the care we showed his daughter and family.

"You are welcome. It was worth all the hours of heartache and deliberation our team experienced to know she has moved forward and is thriving." I ate the rest of my meal in reflective silence, grateful to have the positive closure for this sad chapter of ISK's story.

And the young man? I have no clue how all this translated

into actual learning for him. He surely missed his friends and family back in Kabul, but as a young man in a patriarchal culture, well, he likely moved on in full freedom.

As Afghanistan considers its future, I can only hope it will build on the sacrifices made for women and by women for education and full partnership consideration. Men and women working together, respecting the talents and strengths each brings to the effort, results in a better world for everyone.

The Unveiled Truth: I thought my sacrifice to move to Afghanistan was right and even praiseworthy; I learned it was small compared to so many others who had worked tirelessly and with great personal risk to help women and girls get an education. I am glad to have done what little I could.

We each have one life, one chance to make an impact. We should give our best effort to help others and the world in general when we get the chance.

Whether starting a mud-room school that disappears too soon, helping a troubled teen, or working for change in your own government, your part is needed, vital. Don't wait for someone else to change the world, do what only you can do.

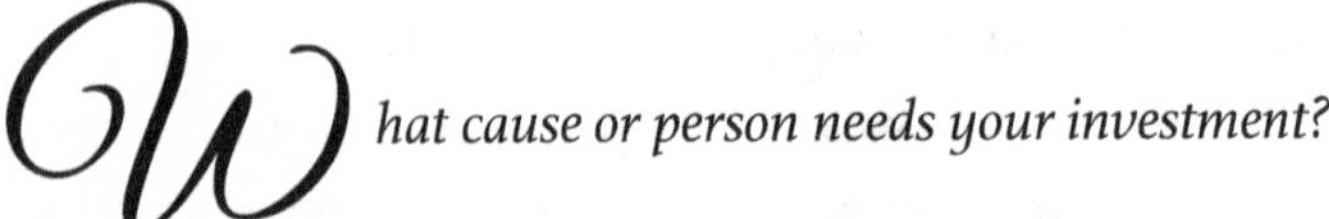

What cause or person needs your investment?

9

Whom Shall I Fear?

"Aren't you afraid to live in Afghanistan?"

I heard that question often, before I moved to Kabul and even after I returned. Usually from Americans who were not global travelers.

Though not a fearful person by nature, I did have to endure two brothers who loved to pop out of nowhere to scare their sisters. I did not watch horror shows late at night while babysitting as a teen or listen to ghost stories around the campfire in my growing-up years as a Girl Scout. These habits plus my cognitive versus emotional nature served me well in an anti-woman, insecure war zone like Afghanistan.

Because Afghan men typically had better English skills, I saw more fathers during my years at ISK than mothers. That fact alone was not a problem. I adored and resembled my own father who had a strong personality. My direct communication style, five foot, nine inch frame, and general self-confidence helped equalize the playing field when negotiating with men. I sometimes even inadvertently intimidated them, which wasn't always an asset but could work for me in a place like Kabul.

Recognizing the low opinion and disrespect of women in Afghanistan, I could have adopted the idea that men, in general, were my enemies. But did I feel fear in their presence?

Not always. Not in my office as the ISK principal. But I was on guard, absolutely. Why?

For one thing, Afghan men know how to persuade and are used to having their way, whether they are common laborers or executives. From their fresh haircuts and heavy aftershave to their pressed shalwar kameez (Afghan traditional clothing for men) or three-piece suits, they presented themselves well in public. Smiling and inquiring about my family and my health, the fathers started conversations with cultural charm.

"How are you, Mrs. Goolsby? And Mr. Goolsby, is he well? And your family back home, do you hear from them often? Thank you for seeing me today." The male visitor would wait to be invited into my office, and I would offer my hand in greeting. He would not have initiated physical contact without my first move.

"How can I help you?" I would ask to make use of my limited time and get to the point of the visit after a brief reciprocal exchange of small talk. My cultural way of conversing, not theirs.

"You are the expert, of course," would be the next comment from my office guest. Ah, I grew to love that statement—something painfully absent from the lips of American parents to school personnel today.

"We are very happy with ISK. Our family is grateful for all you are doing to help educate our children and for bringing such an excellent school to Afghanistan." Other compliments followed. Eventually the true need or concern prompting the appointment would finally enter the conversation.

"You want to take your children out of school for two weeks before the scheduled spring break? Of course, it is your choice, but ISK policy states your children will have zeroes for missed work during unexcused absences. Since this is not an emergency, I suggest you wait for the posted all-school break." I spoke evenly, holding back my sigh of frustration, with a pleasant expression plastered on my face.

The negotiations began. Even though ISK was operating in the Afghan culture, I had to stand firm on our American school academic policies to be the quality school the parents wanted and paid for. Parents tried to press for exceptions to suit their family desires and conveniences which translated into more work for teachers. These bartering sessions with men unused to hearing *no*, especially from a woman, were exhausting. I certainly didn't wish them on my team members.

"You are free to tell families that you cannot make the final decision about student absences," I instructed my team at orientation sessions and before every scheduled school break to relieve them of the coming pressure. "Send them to me."

Holding the line on school policy was not the scariest male encounters I endured. I quaked more when dealing with politically empowered fathers. They knew what they wanted and expected my full submission to their power and position. Some were sons of former Afghan tribal leaders, returning to their country and bringing their Western born children to ISK for education while they served in prestigious government posts.

Or in terrorist organizations, like the Taliban.

"Karen, since Khalid is not available, send for one of the oldest Wardak boys to translate Pashto for me, please." I gestured for the tall, black-turbaned man and his companion to sit in my office chairs. The man's attendant had been relieved of his firearm by an ISK guard upon entering the campus. We waited in silence for a few minutes to have my teen translator arrive. Karen lingered by the open office door with a strained expression after sending for the student.

The student appeared wide-eyed in my doorway, looked at me, then my visitors, then back at me. I motioned for him to come stand by my desk where I sat. The back-and-forth conversation began.

"He has two sons he wants to enroll in ISK, Mrs. Goolsby. They took an English course last year, and he thinks they are ready to study here. He wants them in the same class to help each other." The drafted language assistant did not make eye contact with my visitors during the exchange, only me. I put forward my questions about age, years in school, and why they wanted to attend ISK and received the answers in my student's shaking voice.

After the details had all been laid out, I took a deep breath and chose my words carefully. I needed to hold to ISK standards but try not to offend. Not an easy challenge.

"Thank you for coming in today. We would be glad to assist your family, but unfortunately, at twelve and fourteen years of age, they have not had enough English to succeed at ISK. Both the classes for their ages are full at the present, so I cannot put them in the same class. I am sorry, but it is not possible." I stood and returned the Afghan school documents to the father which, of course, listed them as first in their classes.

When I did not hear the translation of my decision coming forth, I looked over at my student. His mouth was open, his expression clearly shocked. I nodded and he delivered the rejection message in Pashto.

While the two men were escorted out of the building, my student blurted out. "Mrs. Goolsby, you said *no* to a Talib! Aren't you afraid of what he will do?"

"Well, he wants to enroll his children here, why would he blow up the school? But I cannot take in students who will not be successful. How would that make the father happy?" I watched the young man slowly leave my office while shaking his head in disbelief. I guess I should have been afraid, but ISK was my world.

Out on the streets, now that was a different world. I did experience fear there.

From my first visit in 2004 till I left Kabul, I loathed the constant staring by Afghan men on the street. I understood how my daughters and other foreign women felt when they complained of the uneasiness and discomfort the staring produced.

Often groups of Afghan men appeared from seemingly nowhere, forming a crowd to watch a traffic mishap or someone changing a flat tire or a foreign woman shopping on the street. Anytime I walked by such a gathering, even though always accompanied by my husband, a school guard, or a group of teachers, I felt their gazes burning into me.

I determined early on to keep looking straight ahead, never making eye contact with any of them, pretending they were not there. I knew these men would rarely, if ever, touch a foreign woman according to their customs, but I sensed their dislike, maybe even hatred for me. Would they find a way to hurt me? It was a fearful feeling at times, making my heart beat faster than normal until I was home or out of the suffocating urban male crowds.

Daring teen males were more overt, riding their bicycles too close or even right into a group of women as we walked by, hoping to push us into an open sewer or cause us to fall over. Anger replaced fear soon enough at their obnoxious behavior. With glee, I often watched my male companion or guard knock them off their invading bikes or toss rocks into their wheels to avenge me and other female victims. Once, I grabbed my shoe to strike a boy who shouted at me in a threatening manner, not needing a translation of his Dari words to grasp the insults. He ran away.

On the more severe, less common side of this issue, I knew women who were kidnapped, killed, and physically molested by unknown male assailants during my years in Kabul. These events did not always make the news, but word spread throughout ISK and the entire expatriate community in Kabul, causing organizations to enforce stricter safety policies for their women. It became prime requirements for all foreigners, particularly women, to vary their travel paths and not go places alone.

More danger could be found on the overcrowded streets of Kabul than just staring or malicious men. The world outside the ISK compound was chaotic and sometimes volatile.

On Memorial Day 2006, near the end of the first year of ISK, we experienced major fear as afternoon mobs moved toward our campus. An American military truck had crashed into civilian vehicles due to mechanical failure during morning rush-hour traffic in the northern part of the city. A handful of Afghan citizens died, and more were injured. Like sticks of dynamite, tempers flared and quickly ignited groups of disgruntled nationals. Demonstrations and violent crowds moved to various locations in and around Kabul, including the southwest section of town where the Afghan Parliament building and several embassies were located—and ISK.

"Gail, you and Karen stay in front of the admin building

inside the courtyard with all the class rosters." Byron strapped on his full Kevlar body armor and belted on his personal pistol. "No student leaves unless you have the parent's proper identification. The local police are coming to help our guards protect the campus. We've practiced the terrorist drills all year. Now we do it for real." He gave us a nod and then joined the guards outside the school gate but within the security outposts.

Karen was perfect for challenges like this, calm and efficient, alert and sensitive to every need. I squeezed her hand, glad to have her at my side. No words were needed. We gathered our two-way radios and the rosters we always had ready for emergencies and took our positions.

At the signal, the staff moved all two hundred plus ISK students and personnel to designated safe rooms on campus, designed for imminent danger and potentially delayed rescue. We equipped the hidden quarters with water, military food rations, blankets, sleeping mattresses, and battery-operated lanterns. The locations and procedure specifics stayed confidential to the ISK team only, some details such as secret weapons only known to select senior leadership personnel.

Everyone responded perfectly, moving quickly and quietly. Students took cues from their teachers that this was not a drill. Mobile phones flashed messages from family members to children, causing the cell tower system to overload that day. Staff kept their young charges busy with whisper-level activities. Teenagers sat in silent stress, having fuller comprehension of the situation.

"Smell that, Karen? Something's burning." I stood close to her in the eerie empty school courtyard and gripped my clipboard like it was a shield. We both recognized the sound of multiple gunshots as the protestors marched down Darluman

Avenue toward Parliament, a mere quarter of a mile away from ISK. We later learned a local pizza shop was vandalized and set on fire two blocks away.

Within about thirty minutes, stressed parents began to trickle in toward us after extra-tight security scrutiny at ISK gates.

"Mrs. Goolsby, the people are crazy out there. I am so thankful for ISK's security. I want to get my children home as quickly as possible, please." I nodded and checked the British mother's students off the roster. Karen radioed the teachers of the boys to release them to the office. We continued this procedure for several hours.

Many high-level government parents were sequestered deep down in security bunkers with no way to communicate, so relatives called to let us know of their delays in picking up their children. Karen and I kept detailed messages and counted student departures using our radios, following the lockdown procedure, bypassing blocked cell phones.

When Byron finally returned to the admin building, he gave Karen and me one of his friendly winks. Smiling back, I let relief wash over me. All was okay. The three of us hugged and leaned into each other for a few minutes. No parent had been hurt on route to ISK. Every student had been delivered safely to his or her family.

Later it was determined most of the rioters were young men, even schoolchildren, with rocks and sticks, unhappy with present living conditions and looking to blame foreigners, police, government, or anyone they deemed responsible for current problems.

"I am totally exhausted," my twenty-something first-grade teacher remarked to me as she entered the dining hall with the other team members. "I will never forget this day, will you?"

Many staff members' heads joined mine in shaking a firm *no,* never. I felt the side effects of the tense afternoon, stiffness in my jaw from clenching my teeth and aching leg and back muscles from standing and walking for hours without sitting or resting. ISK fared well with no intruders and no incidents on our campus. We gratefully ate our delayed dinner, kept warm for us by our caring Sakhi.

Later that night, we met together in the Marble Mansion basement recreation lounge.

"Today was incredibly stressful, but you all did so well. Let's talk about this. What did you see and feel through this event?" I looked intently at my brave team as Byron and I led the debrief. "We need to release our overwhelmed emotions so let's start tonight. It will help, believe me. And then you can continue to share with your coworkers and roommates in the days to come as needed."

After impressive tales of student cooperation, there were some humorous kindergarten anecdotes, which let laughter have its healing place. Staff commented that they could still smell smoke and hear gunshots in their minds. And that they felt the weight of responsibility to protect students in a new, heavier way now. The unscripted discussion continued for more than an hour.

"Okay, this is a great response. Keep talking to each other. Gail and I are available for private conversations, too." Byron motioned to Karen to take a marker and move toward a large whiteboard in the room. "Now let's list any mistakes and needed changes for next time. That is our new reality, folks. It happened once; it could happen again."

Byron and I took the team's feedback to the next morning's admin meeting, which included our security manager, a former special forces-trained soldier or policeman.

"It's like *shooting in the dark*, almost literally," Byron complained at the meeting. "Nothing stays the same in this crazy city. Who's mad at President Karzai or George W. Bush today? Who's in charge of the government today? Aargh!" He slapped his desk in frustration when our security manager outlined changes, yet again, for campus safety after the recent incident.

While the men outside our gates might represent danger, the men inside the ISK compound were powerful barriers to fear overtaking my peace of mind. In addition to the security manager, we relied heavily on our highly trained national guards. Throughout the day and night, rotations of guards came and went on the ISK campus. We appreciated these men, many husbands and fathers themselves, who picked up their weapons and donned bulletproof vests daily to keep us safe.

They focused keenly on morning and afternoon car-line procedures as our twelve-foot street gates were opened and the campus became vulnerable. Car windshields displayed uniquely designed and numbered ISK tags assigned to each family and vehicle. These tags were changed each year and, if lost, required a replacement fee to discourage casualness about this security plan. Public taxis were not allowed on campus. These vehicles, or others who forgot the car tag, had to unload their precious student cargo on side streets beyond our protection.

We did not engage our guards in long conversations. They each had an important job to do and needed to remain vigilant at all times. But my people-focused husband memorized all the men's names every year and greeted them personally whenever they opened the gate for our entry or exit from campus. He learned early on the common small talk and the custom to place his hand on his heart with a slight head nod when greeting one another. They loved *Mr. Mike* as they respectfully called him.

As the principal of ISK, I was always acknowledged as *Mrs. Goolsby* with a slight bow of respect and softly spoken salutations. I returned, "Salaam," with a smile, but with very brief eye contact, as custom dictated between unrelated men and women. Like our national maintenance crew, I felt very safe under the care of these Afghan men.

Negative experiences and dangerous events caused me to pursue fewer excursions off campus over time. That is not the healthiest balance when you work and live in the same compound. It also worked against sustaining general positive regard for the men on the street, although I did not allow myself to foster hate in my heart for all strangers. I would not accept that every man was full of evil intent, but I never felt totally free of fear and concern out there.

I knew I could not stay long-term in Afghanistan with a negative, pessimistic, fearful outlook. All seven years that I lived there, it was a constant challenge to stay open, to believe the best, to forgive men who didn't know better than to behave like the brutes before them, and to resist fear when danger came crashing into my world. But it was a challenge I took up because I believed God had sent me to Afghanistan to help teach the students at ISK, and God used the experience to teach me as well.

The Unveiled Truth: 2 Timothy 1:7 (ASV) says: *For God gave us not a spirit of fearfulness; but of power and love and discipline.* That is what I wanted while I was in

Afghanistan: power and a disciplined mind to separate paranoia from reality. I knew that would serve me well anytime fear tempted me to give in and give up.

We should prepare, plan, and do our best to reduce dangerous or worrisome circumstances, but we cannot control everything or everyone. We have to have faith, to trust that God is present, all powerful, and will deliver us somehow, someway. As the Sovereign overall, God wins, not evil.

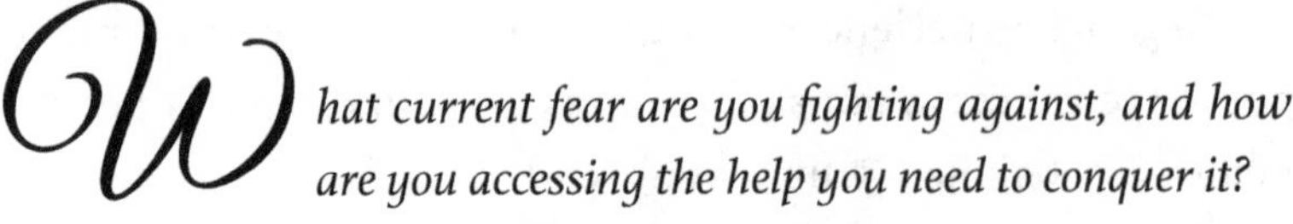

hat current fear are you fighting against, and how are you accessing the help you need to conquer it?

10

Surviving Deep Waters

I've been a leadership aficionado from a young age, maybe because I was the oldest daughter and had siblings to look after. In high school and college, both Michael and I participated in youth leadership groups and activities. We met at a conference in Orlando during our college years in the late 70s, serving as young leaders for our different national organizations.

In my married years, I pioneered groups and programs in our churches, communities, and at work in the various places we lived. Leadership always drew me, as a study and in practice. I enjoyed the challenges and the potential to help others. Often, I found myself in a middle-leader position, which can be the most challenging as one must serve both those above and below, but I learned how to navigate this tricky organizational position and felt comfortable there.

In Kabul, as a brand-new principal at an international

school, I knew I was in over my head. Add the whole male-superiority culture weighing in on me as a foreign female leader and the waters felt deep and dangerous. As an educator, counselor, and pastor's wife, I was aware of the dynamics of team-leader relationships and the importance of doing it correctly, especially overseas. Living and working on a closed compound sounded like a doomsday set-up for all of us. I didn't want people leaving Afghanistan because of an unhealthy team environment.

Even with the professional endorsement my Missouri colleagues and friends offered to the Oasis organization that led to my being hired for this position, I wanted desperately to have training and mentoring for my new role. I can be honest about not knowing things, but that will not work for very long when you are the leader. When I refused the ISK Director role from Oasis in early 2005—accepting the principal job instead—I prayed, fasted, and hoped for a wonderful working relationship with my boss-to-be.

"You must be the Goolsbys."

I turned around from my seat at the Memphis Redbirds baseball stadium to check out the voice. The entire group from the Oasis summer Pre-Field Orientation had taken the night off from training to enjoy the minor league sporting event. Michael and I were sitting apart from the rest of the group to stay cool in the humid weather and chat about PFO out of public earshot.

"And you must be Dr. Greene." I smiled and reached out to shake his hand. "I wondered when we would meet." I had heard Byron was hired as the ISK Director two months earlier, but he had not attended the first week of PFO with the rest of the Kabul team. I took in the handsome face and neatly trimmed salt-and-pepper goatee that matched his full head of hair. I guessed Byron to be about the same age we were, near fifty.

"I had some family things that delayed my coming. Call me Byron. I'll be around the next few days meeting with Joe Hale and others to get curriculum ordered and review some rental property paperwork for the school. You won't see me in the conference sessions since that's not my priority. But you keep doing what you're doing to get the ISK folks ready to leave next month." He leaned forward in his seat and continued this one-way conversation for about fifteen minutes while Michael and I strained our necks to maintain eye-contact behind us.

"This is how it's gonna work. I will oversee the complicated budget, USAID paperwork, the security, and getting us connected with the Afghan government. Gail, you will run the school and head up accreditation, which we need to jump on immediately. We need the credibility with the government and for our students who will be transferring and graduating."

"Do you wanna come sit with us?" I asked Byron when there was a break in his comments. Michael and I moved down a couple of seats to make room for Byron to join our row and make it easier to talk. Other ISK staff started looking our direction and I planned to introduce him to the team.

"No, I'm not staying. Gotta go. Just wanted to greet you and Michael and say I'm really glad to have you coming to Kabul. We have lots to do to get this school going in a short time. Need good people like you two, and since you've already experienced Afghanistan, you are vital." He gave my husband a hearty pat on the shoulder and then looked at me. "You don't look like I pictured, Gail. And I mean that in a good way." With a smile and a wink, Byron got up and left.

I looked at Michael in stunned silence. Finally, I managed to blurt out, "What's up with him? How do you just drop big statements like that in a first meeting? Why isn't he engaging with our team more? And what do you think he meant by I 'don't look like he pictured'?"

I could feel irritation mounting as I mentally listed Byron's errors in this first meet-up.

Knowing me well, Michael put his arm around me and said quietly, but firmly, "It will be all right, you'll see. Don't overthink things and make premature judgments. Wait till we all get to Kabul and become better acquainted."

I could not focus on the baseball game after that encounter with my new boss. On the bus returning to PFO lodgings, ISK staff came up to ask me if that had been Dr. Greene and what he was like. I had little information to settle their curiosity but tried to be positive for the team and for myself.

Byron's expectations about my role at ISK while at the baseball game succeeded in overwhelming me. I did not even know what questions to ask and whether he even wanted me to ask them. When back home, I requested the administrative assistant at St. Joseph Christian School to put all handbooks, accreditation materials, and other forms and documents on computer discs for me to take to Kabul. I desperately wanted all the help I could get, unsure my new boss would supply what I needed considering he hadn't seemed eager to spend any time with me planning for how things should go.

From our first days in Afghanistan, Byron demonstrated he knew exactly what was needed to start a new school. I was impressed and happily followed his directions as we brainstormed vision statements, core values, and even logos for ISK. The team was eager and talented, so these were energizing sessions.

There were surprises, too. Our first year, and every August

orientation thereafter, he'd tell the teachers, "If you need to talk about some kiddo who isn't performing or supplies that are needed for a great lesson you want to teach, her office is down the hall." He gestured toward me and out the door. "Don't come to me about that stuff. I don't want to hear about it."

I read the surprise and apprehension on the staff faces looking at their director. His statements proved true, for he doggedly stayed within his identified areas of responsibility and trusted me with the rest during our time in Kabul—almost to a fault.

During the first two years, Byron made lots of trips to the U.S. and other places. He did not require or want my permission to be gone from campus. I understood that. I was not his boss. He had his reasons and they were reasonable—spending time with his wife back in America, supporting his son during his senior year of high school, attending international school leadership conferences, and staying connected with other educational peers.

But the consequences of his frequent trips created a lot of stress on me. I wanted him around as I learned to navigate my unique position as a female principal in a man's world and made that clear to him on several occasions, in mild and not-so mild tones. "But what about the parent meetings coming up? And the visit from the Minister of Education? You know they want to see *you*, not me."

He left anyway and kept reminding me how much he trusted me to take care of things.

In the early years, my confidence was not up to the level of his expectations. If it hadn't been for Khalid, Michael, Karen, and other seasoned senior administrative team members, I would not have lasted. Byron and I never established a regular time for training as I'd hoped, rather we had sporadic *mentoring moments* as I called them.

"So, I believe principals need to be MBWA, Gail." Byron appeared in my office one day in our first year with a fresh cup of coffee from the break room down the hall.

"What does that mean?" I stopped looking for the email I needed and gazed at him quizzically.

"Management by walking around." He made himself comfortable in one of my office chairs. "The staff and students need to see you more. Spend at least a third of your time being present in classrooms and all over campus. Let the teachers and students get used to you dropping in so they stay on their toes. That way, people don't freak out when they see you, worried that there's trouble. Makes for more congenial relationships." He stood to leave. "One more thing. Before you leave your office, always plaster a big smile on your face. When everyone sees their principal's happy, they love their school even more." He gave me a wink and a nod of confidence, then left as quickly as he came in.

Byron was hard to pin down between his travel and meetings off campus, but he faithfully took my phone calls, let me interrupt him in his office, and answered my emails. His written responses were short since he typed with two fingers and only learned to use Microsoft Office when he came to Kabul. (In his previous positions, he had enjoyed efficient personally assigned administrative assistants who made his verbal ideas and directives look great on paper.) I learned early on to only ask one question per email because then I knew what the "yes" or "no" response applied to.

Once when Joe Hale came to Kabul to visit, I communicated my complaints about Byron's absences from campus. He listened, and then, to my dissatisfaction, replied, "Well, Gail, I guess you need to decide if you would rather have him as little as you do, versus not at all." I took no comfort from that advice.

I never had to guess if Byron was pleased or frustrated with me, though. When I did a good job, he let me know in brief but meaningful comments either in person or email. And when I was in trouble, he let me know that, too.

One day, I had set up an appointment to review a stack of pressing issues I felt needed his wisdom and support before deciding what to do. I knocked and walked into his office when he said, "Come in."

Upon opening the door, I realized someone else was there that I didn't know. I stood with my hand on the doorknob. I could see by the tray of coffee and sweets that he was entertaining an ISK guest. *On my time.*

"Hey, Gail, this is Susan. She is a journalist visiting Kabul. I invited her to come see the campus in case she wants to do a story about ISK."

At Byron's introduction, Susan rose to shake my hand and smile in friendly greeting. I gave her a perfunctory nod and handshake.

I turned to address Byron in flat tones. "I thought we were meeting?"

"Yep, right, but we'll have to do it later. So, Susan went to an international school herself. I'm going to show her around now." He rose from his desk chair, grabbed his coat, and looked at me, "Want to join us?"

I shot him a dark look and left his office.

I slammed the pile of notes and papers on my desk and closed my door, which I rarely did in order to indicate an open-door policy with my staff. If the door was closed, that meant a private meeting was happening. This day it was to privately vent and even pout.

I can't believe he did this to me again. How am I supposed to learn how to do this job better if I can't get any focused attention? I am not high maintenance. I am working hard, but good grief, once in a while I need my boss to help me.

My self-pity cloud lifted as I lost myself in returning parent calls and reviewing teacher lesson plans. Thirty minutes later, Byron walked into my office and closed the door. I turned from my computer and saw him standing directly in front of my desk, his hands on his hips. *Uh-oh.*

"That thing you did in there," he pointed toward his office, "I better never see that again." His face was flushed and his eyes intense. The usual smile lines around his eyes were absent. "I was totally embarrassed in front of a guest. You acted like a child."

Where a few minutes earlier my own anger might have matched his, now I could only nod in acquiescence. He stood glaring at me a few minutes longer.

"I apologize. You are right. I acted badly." I spoke quietly but looked him in the eye. "I just..." I started to excuse my immature behavior but thought better of it and shut up.

Byron sat down across from me. "I know you wanted to meet, and we will. Today, I promise. But you have to be flexible. You know that. You teach that to your team."

We sat in silence, gently watching each other. "Are we good?" Byron finally asked.

I nodded, suddenly wanting to go home and cry. Some principal I was. My gaze dropped to my lap as I struggled to hold back tears. Byron rose and patted my shoulder. "None of us are perfect. I'm surely not. I know I don't always do right by you, I get that. But haven't you figured out my principal training mantra by now?"

I shook my head, daring to look up at him. His smile lines were back, and I sensed a cheesy pun coming my way, another thing he was known for, to the delight of my husband and Khalid.

"Throw 'em in water over their head and just let 'em swim. I've done that with a few principals in my tenure and it worked out well. It's working well for you, too. You are doing a great job, don't think otherwise." With another friendly pat, he headed out my door.

Byron never presented himself as perfect, but he did not present much doubt about his actions either, just confidence. The same observation about my lack of doubt in my abilities has been made about me over the years, and not usually as a compliment.

On one significant staff evaluation for our accreditation requirements, the results showed that many of our staff believed us both to be *poor listeners with little compassion for others.*

Some of my ISK teachers felt about me the same way I often felt about my boss. Ouch.

While reviewing this feedback alone with Byron, I took the criticism to heart, seeking counsel on how to improve. I related how one of my trusted educator mentors had talked me through the evaluation results, offered suggestions for improvement, and recommended some helpful books by successful school leaders.

Byron listened to my concerns and offered some constructive thoughts for my growth, but in regard to his own evaluation, he basically said, "Yep, that's me."

At the end of our third school year, on June 1, 2008, I had to come to grips with the possibility of leading ISK without Byron. He went mountain climbing one morning (a popular hobby with our staff until security became a problem) and had a major heart attack, severe enough to be dubbed "the widow maker." He could have easily died if he hadn't pushed himself to go back down the mountain, enduring the intense pain, but breaking up the fatal blockage in the process.

After stabilizing him with the limited available emergency help through a blur of decisions and details, we got him medevacked to Dubai. Michael and I visited him a week later as he was recuperating for release to fly home to the U.S.

As I left him, I felt overwhelmed but grateful to still have him. I didn't want to lose him, especially by a heart attack on a dusty Afghan mountain. In my mind and heart, I repented of all my complaints.

Byron made a good recovery and planned to return to ISK in August 2008 for one last year. His family and American doctor did not understand his reasons for wanting to go back. I, however, breathed a sigh of relief. I determined to make sure he took care of himself while back in Kabul, keep him from working too hard, and make the most of the mentoring moments we had left.

My graceful thoughts quickly dissipated when he kept delaying his actual arrival and avoiding communication with me. In typical Byron fashion, he decided to spend some extra days with friends in Dubai on his way back to Afghanistan in August, leaving me to get the school ready to open on my own. Familiar frustration rose within me and pushed gratitude out of the picture.

"What are you upset about? You know how to get the school started without him. You've done it every year anyway.

He basically just shows up for his welcome speech." Michael tried to reason me out of my tantrum.

"He knows how important the Back-to-School event is to kick off the school year. All the parents, mostly fathers, come to see the *main man*, the director. They all know about Byron's heart attack and want to see him well again, and with their own eyes. And he isn't going to be here." I plopped onto my bedroom chair and sat there in the dark for a long time, making myself more miserable by the hour.

In truth, I didn't need Byron. He had given me what I needed by throwing me into the churning chaos, yet like well-timed life preservers flung my direction, he didn't forget to offer me those mentoring moments when the water was about to overtake me. His hands-off style of supervision appeared non-caring and even selfish at times, but for a self-starter leader-type like me, it worked, even when I didn't realize it.

I planned the school program and, as usual, had plenty of administrative help, timed the large group presentations with classroom tours, and prepared all the remarks I typically shared as the principal plus Byron's announcements easily enough. Everything went well and I was not nervous in the least. After all the times I'd led ISK by myself in the past three years, plus what I learned completing another master's degree in Educational Leadership while in Kabul, I'd found my confidence.

It was a turning point. I could swim these waters alone.

In October 2008, a formal press event was planned to document ISK's official recognition by the Afghanistan Ministry of Education. The current Minister Hanif Atmar had been a good friend to ISK in our early years when we were held in suspicion, and even contempt, by the traditional Afghan educational leaders. It was a very big deal.

And wouldn't you know it, Byron was not going to be in-country.

"Are you going to be okay with this?" Byron brought me into his office to discuss the upcoming ceremony and his absence. "Khalid will be with you, of course."

"You know what? I'm fine. Even though I was unsure in the beginning how I could head up our accreditation, I did it. We all did it, and I'll proudly, even confidently, represent us at the signing ceremony." I sat across from my boss and smiled in peace and appreciation. I had come a long way in feeling comfortable as a principal.

I didn't drown during the countless times Byron threw me in over my head at ISK. God gave me what I needed to keep my head above water, from my past education and leadership experiences to a great team. I learned to swim just fine and gained not only confidence but satisfaction in my work.

In retrospect, we actually made a good leadership team, Byron and I, even with, or in spite of, our strong personalities.

The Unveiled Truth: As a life coach, I tell my clients the answers to their transitions and challenges are inside of them. My job is to assist them in creating their own problem-solving, goal-achieving strategies.

At the beginning of new endeavors, we can feel like we are drowning in uncertainty, and there's no shame in needing help. But we often think we need a certain kind of help and may be too stubborn to take advantage of what is provided.

When you're in deep waters, keep treading intentionally and working to move forward. Trust that God will throw a life preserver when, or if, you actually need it, not just because you're tired or scared. Sometimes you need to develop muscles and stamina on your own, which provides for the present and prepares you for any rough seas ahead.

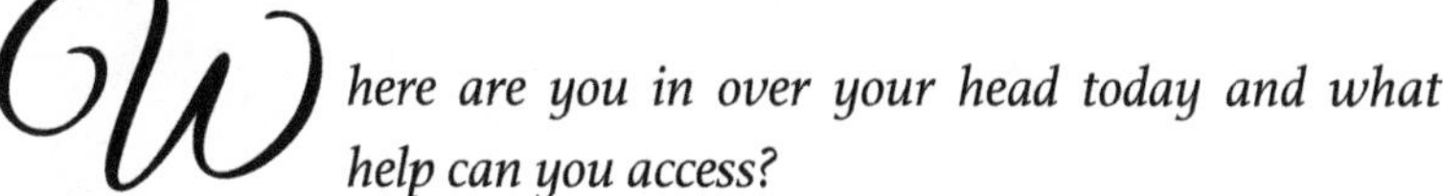

here are you in over your head today and what help can you access?

11

Safety is Overrated

AFGHANISTAN - LEVEL 4: DO NOT TRAVEL.

"Travel to all areas of Afghanistan is unsafe because of critical levels of kidnappings, hostage taking, suicide bombings, widespread military combat operations, landmines, and terrorist and insurgent attacks, including attacks using vehicle-borne, magnetic, or other improvised explosive devices (IEDs), suicide vests, and grenades."

This post appeared on the U.S. State Department travel information website and the U.S. Embassy Afghanistan homepage in April 2019. We saw the same warning in 2005 when we moved to Kabul. The news reports beginning in September 2001 contained startling information and scary photos about fighting, bombing, death, and the general danger of Afghanistan. Our family and friends expressed their dismay over our decision to relocate to this war-decimated and poverty-stricken place.

"A copy of our wills is here in the filing cabinet." Michael showed our children where our legal papers were kept in the basement of our Missouri home. It was the same weekend we had the burial versus cremation discussion before we left for Kabul. "There is another copy in our safety deposit box along with the car and house deeds and power of attorney forms. Everything is in order and Mr. Horman will help you if anything happens to us. He has a key to the bank box and a copy of the wills, too." Michael closed the file cabinet and looked at our oldest daughter with compassion. His father's heart was in turmoil.

Sarah nodded her head but said nothing. Her wide-eyed stare spoke clearly how incredulous this conversation seemed to her. But we knew that under the precarious conditions of Afghanistan, all these documents were necessary. The U.S. State Department website still outlines twelve specific points for these types of pre-travel preparations today.

"Will you be safe?"

"We'll be praying for your safety."

Close friends and mere acquaintances felt compelled to say such when they heard about our plans to move to Kabul.

As I lived month after month, year after year in Afghanistan, I began to develop a vastly different opinion about the value, the almost birthright view, of safety held by Westerners. I came to realize that people born in other parts of the world rarely considered safety as their first priority.

Though many native families didn't seem to place safety as their top concern, as a school with students coming every day, Byron and I needed to provide secure measures for those under our care. ISK spent time, energy, and much money on safety plans and resources, not only once, but continually. Other families came to ISK specifically because it met the strict security they required in their government or business positions.

Each August, we slotted in a full morning session during team orientation week for new and returning staff members to cover personal safety and lockdown procedures. The training opened any naïve minds to the reality of living in Kabul. We discussed the reasons for the various color-coded levels of restricted travel in the city and how the restrictions were assessed.

"Here is how you sign-out." Byron showed the clipboard during orientation which was kept by the ISK drivers' station. "You cannot just leave campus. You must request a driver and time, plus record exactly where you will be going. Check the vetted list of places and then try to go in groups to economize our drivers and vehicles." He passed the clipboard around to familiarize staff with the procedure.

"If I buy a bicycle, can I go places on my own? The Afghan workers use them. I can take care of myself." I looked to see who was asking this question. Our new PE teacher sat with his arms crossed and a tight expression.

Hmm, is he going to be trouble?

Well, yes, he did push the boundaries often in his one year at ISK, scribbling only "out" on the information log and disappearing by bicycle for hours on the weekends. Neither Byron nor I could obtain his cooperation on this safety requirement.

Each year, the faces and remarks of the younger staff communicated their opinions of these safeguards—excessive and unnecessary. They were used to driving, living on their own, answering only to themselves, and few restrictions. That was not our situation in Kabul. Some teachers left or were released based on their inability to cooperate with these limitations, like the free-wheeling PE guy.

When staff pushback came, Byron continually gave the response these invincible young adults hated to hear. I agreed with every word he barked with his hands on his hips in a commanding posture and a stern expression on his face.

"I don't want to make a call to your family that you've been hurt or even killed while at ISK. Not on my watch! We are here to run a school and we need every one of you here every day. We will err on the conservative side and send you home in one piece at the end of your time here. End of discussion."

Only four months into our time in Kabul, we were forced to recognize that even our best security plans could not cover all possible threats to our safety.

It was the end of November, our first fall in Kabul in 2005. The explosion that pierced the night's silence shook our campus and knocked the clock off our bedroom wall at three-thirty a.m.

"What happened?" I cried out to Michael, who did not instantly wake up since he doesn't wear his hearing aids to bed. I shook him as I jumped out of bed. "I think the boiler in the Marble Mansion blew up!"

I raced in panic to our window overlooking the shared courtyard and attempted to open the curtains, only to realize glass was falling in and stopped. Michael and I threw on robes and coats and went outside to check on staff and count noses.

"Where is Charlene?" I screeched to Karen as soon as I saw her come out of the Marble Mansion. I knew our librarian's bedroom was on the main floor just above the enormous heater-boiler that I had imagined exploding. However, nothing looked out of the ordinary except broken glass everywhere. Soon I saw Charlene with my own eyes and wiped away tears before she even knew of my unfounded concern.

"Make a list. Check that everyone is here. Where are Byron

and Creighton?" I gave the paper and pen I'd carried down from my apartment to Karen. We collected the team together from the other campus houses and sighed our relief at no injuries. Then we tried to piece together what had happened.

Byron and his son, Creighton, who was visiting from America, soon entered our courtyard with animated expressions. They had followed the smoke billowing into the early morning sky after the explosion to the compound next door to the Marble Mansion and our apartment. I could not see over the walls but heard the commotion of many Dari voices.

"The property next door is decimated, including their car. A huge crater shows where the thing hit. Lots of pressure, not much fire." Byron checked my list of staff all accounted for and nodded his head in approval.

Creighton continued with teenage enthusiasm, "I jumped into the hole. The guy was laying on his bed right beside where the bomb landed and he walked away. He can't hear anything, but he isn't dead! So cool! I took pics on my phone. Want to see?" He started to scroll through photos to show interested staff.

Local Afghan police as well as ISAF (International Security Assistance Force) officers soon arrived on the scene and gave us more details. That night, four Russian mortars landed in locations around Kabul. The military reports concluded the attacks *may* have been intended by the Taliban or another political group to hit specific city targets, but the old mortars were famous for errors. The neighbors believed their misfortune was ISK's fault since we were Americans, even though there was never any proof.

"I need to go with my guys to check all the buildings and assess the damage." Michael hugged me and gathered the Afghan maintenance men that were now arriving, hours before their usual shifts. Byron and Creighton went along as well, no doubt for more pics the teen could send to his buddies back home in Georgia. Clearly he thought he was having one great adventure.

"Let's go to the Marble Mansion and get some coffee." I led the huddled group of bathrobed staff into the living room of the large dorm.

"I just got a text from the Harrison family," Karen announced as we started heating water for tea and French press coffee. It was a couple of hours into our ordeal. "They want someone to come to the end of the street to meet them. The police won't let them on campus, but they have trays of homemade cinnamon rolls for us." She and another teacher went into their rooms to throw on full-length coats and head-scarves to collect the yummy care package.

The whole team was shaken up from this experience, some more than others. I worried that some would choose to leave. I arranged for critical incident debriefing exercises with local experienced international workers.

"A couple of your single women and one family said they would leave if something like that mortar blast happens again." One of the facilitators sat in my office and reported to me significant staff member conversations from the debrief. I nodded in understanding. My own children were wanting the same commitment from Michael and me. I wasn't sure how I felt about the event. I really didn't have much time to reflect as I scurried to care for everyone and get the school reopened.

"What have we got, Michael?" Byron asked as the three of us gathered to walk the campus the day after the blast. Glass was everywhere and school had to be suspended for safety and clean-up.

"Well, all the windows and doors, many in weak wooden

frames without caulk or secure fittings, took the worst of the explosion. We missed the mark by only having bomb blast film on windows facing the street. Every bit of glass on every building needs that extra protection. See how the busted windows with film stay together?" Michael pointed to a pile of extracted panes, all cracked and broken but in one large piece, held by the strong plastic adhesive. "The guards are hearing from neighbors located two or three blocks away who incurred damage from the blast. That is how forceful the pressure was in that mortar." We all shook our heads in wonder.

"How will we be sure every bit of glass is out of the rugs in the classrooms?" I asked Michael as we checked the kindergarten room. "We can't bring the students back until we know no one will be cut. You know how the little ones sit on the carpet and most of our students wear sandals or go barefoot in their classrooms well into November."

"Working on it. My guys are being extremely careful. Brought in the whole crew, even those who weren't scheduled. We are moving as fast as we can while still making it safe for the kids and teachers." Michael hurried off to answer questions to workers awaiting his direction.

One of the most memorable pieces from this crisis was the response of our national staff. Michael and I still recall how we felt when one Afghan worker after another refused to go home after the explosion, even when their shift was over.

Ali told Michael and me in his broken English with great emotion, "My place is here. This should not happen to you. You left your beautiful country to come and teach our children." I waited silently for him to finish though I was too choked to respond anyway. For a moment, Ali made eye contact with me, culturally unheard of, but in this dire situation, totally appropriate. We were just humans caught in the same horrific experience, needing to bond together for the strength and will to get to the other side of the trauma.

"This is what we know in Afghanistan. You should not have these bad things happen." Ali picked up a broom and gathered a wheelbarrow to continue collecting the broken glass and debris around our apartment courtyard.

I watched him go, deeply touched by his declarations of loyalty and support, along with Noorullah, his brother Habib, and the other workers. This was not the first time I had noted with admiration the resilience and determination of Afghans to keep living each day, no matter what happened.

We opened school four days after the assault and understood a little of what the Afghans had been enduring for four decades. Crisis, clean-up, and continue onward. We thankfully never had another mortar blast. I did not experience nightmares, but grew more sensitive to the sounds of explosions after our incident, even benign ones like the supervised destruction of unearthed land mines by international safety crews that happened Tuesdays at noon on a Kabul mountain.

I hoped I would not have to expand my knowledge of safety and security beyond ISK. That was Byron's responsibility more than mine. But during my first year, I received an invitation from the U.S. Consulate in Kabul to serve as a warden for our large group of Americans at ISK. Wardens help the Embassy keep tabs on American citizens throughout the country. I was directed to distribute brochures for citizen-abroad registration with the U.S. Embassy in Kabul so that every staff member would have direct access to security information and relevant warnings.

Byron sometimes attended the warden meetings with me.

He did a great job making sure the powers that be were aware of ISK's presence, our service in Kabul, and our vulnerability. Whenever he could, Byron initiated campus visits by State Department employees and attended Embassy and USAID events to meet people who could help ISK with security and finances. He intentionally socialized with these influential decision-makers to make connections for school resources and staff morale needs.

"Send an email, Gail, to everyone about a barbeque Friday night. ISAF is inviting the ISK team to their base to enjoy shrimp, burgers, and steak off the grill. I will line up our school van and other vehicles. Get a headcount." Byron dropped a memo on my desk with the details and left my office.

I crafted the happy email. We needed fun outings like this off campus. The tight security at ISAF (International Security Assistance Force) took some time clearing, but proved to be a great, safe opportunity for us to learn about other countries' investment in Afghanistan through military and humanitarian efforts.

As we made friendships on the handful of Kabul military bases, teachers found generous offers for overseas shipping help, opportunities to shop at the commissaries, and other fun activities. Occasionally soldiers came to school to share their musical talents or teach a science lesson or read books to eager elementary students in Miss Crump's library. One ISK teacher eventually married a U.S. serviceman she met in Kabul through weekly military chapel services!

I learned a lot about the U.S. government's work overseas as I attended warden meetings and other Embassy gatherings.

And the one message that came across loud and clear to

me and Byron: *we were not guaranteed rescue or evacuation help should we need it at ISK.*

There was the vague assurance that everything possible would be done, but, nothing was promised or put into writing. That made us nervous.

In his bulldog fashion, Byron hunted out other avenues to meet the safety needs of hundreds of ISK children and staff in insecure Kabul.

"Gail, meet CT." Byron brought a muscled, smiling hulk of a man into my office one day in our first years in Kabul. "He works for Blackwater USA. Show him around ISK." Byron clapped the visitor on the back and gestured my direction. "She's the real boss, you know. I'm just for show." He went into his office and left me to start the tour as I did for all ISK visitors.

"Thanks for your time," CT said as we ended the campus visit. "I have seen many Afghan schools in my years here. You guys have done an amazing job and clearly are doing the real thing here. Impressive. Let me know if you need any help from us." He shook my hand and gave me a warm smile before getting into his armored, chauffeured vehicle. CT and other Blackwater personnel made many visits to ISK, and we enjoyed their personal attention and support.

The private security forces men we met were family-oriented, considerate, highly trained ex-soldiers who cared deeply about the outcome of the war in Afghanistan. Blackwater USA supported a family of three students to study at ISK for several years. They flew our school's dance studio floor weighing hundreds of pounds over from Omaha in their cargo plane, for free! They designed an emergency plan for our campus, should such a drastic need arise, to help all our team be evacuated safely. That plan only lasted while Blackwater remained in Kabul, but we felt better prepared to face the unknown crises for several years.

Many of our ISK fathers offered another layer of security assistance. One of our dads headed the President Protective Services for President Karzai, and others worked with the Afghan National Security Forces and the National Directorate of Security. Still others were top-level military officers. I knew they cared about what happened on our campus, after all, their own precious sons and daughters were here.

I told Karen more than once, "If you see some of these guys' kids absent from school, alert me. They know more of what is going on than we do, I'm sure of it." A couple of times I was summoned by one of these dads to discuss the security measures at ISK. They needed us to continue operating for the sake of educating their children. We needed their information to stay open and safe.

Risk and safety concerns were a daily topic, never going away during my ISK years. In our modern age, I had the capability almost twenty-four seven to communicate with folks back home through cell calls, text messages, or email whenever news flashes indicated trouble in Kabul. Sometimes I had to chuckle that Americans knew about Kabul incidents before I did. CNN, BBC, and FOX news had seemingly instant notifications of problems, whereas I had to wait for local security updates.

That easily accessible information was not always helpful in the hands of people living outside of Afghanistan. Sometimes the risk or damage assessment sent over the airwaves did not measure up to my reality. Since I was actually living in the vicinity of the disturbance, I felt there was often exaggeration or other misrepresentations of the crisis. Frequently, I had to make assurances to my children and supporters that things were not as bad as the media presented.

But sometimes it was truly terrible news. Like the mortar blast. Like the Memorial Day demonstrations. Like the explosions and kidnappings and break-ins and murders happening to foreigners—people I knew personally.

But in the midst of busy school life and with our dedicated guards and safety plans in place, I did not think about danger all the time. But I couldn't deny that risk was part of my life in Kabul every day.

Still, safety did not drive my decision about living and remaining in Afghanistan. I chose to fulfill my call, to trust God for what happened and that He would lead me through any crisis. I could have left after my first two-year contract was completed. However, I stayed for almost five more years, making peace with the risks.

The Unveiled Truth: In Afghanistan, I was stretched and stressed. I was sometimes afraid, but not enough to quit and leave, which was an option at any time for most foreigners in Kabul. I chose instead to press through, like the Afghans all around me. I learned many lessons about what I could handle, one being we don't have to feel *safe* to grow and thrive.

When we make safety our first priority, we may exclude opportunities to experience life on a truly transformational level. We may miss the chance of a lifetime to understand new cultures, the global impact of our talents and abilities, and indeed, what inner strength and resiliency we possess.

Check your own safety thermometer. If you are dismissing

a viable possibility to learn, grow, and give because it holds risk, perhaps you should rethink, plan well, take a deep breath, and go for it.

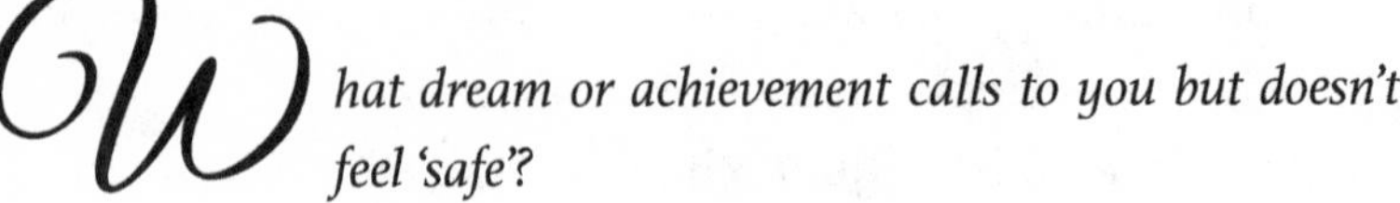

What dream or achievement calls to you but doesn't feel 'safe'?

12

Don't Judge a Book (or a Librarian) by its Cover

The night of the mortar explosion in November 2005 taught me many things about safety and risk and their shifting priority in my life. The shocking event also caused me to realize my growing affection for the people now woven into my daily life, who only a few months earlier had been total strangers.

During that early morning panic, I realized I did not want to be in Kabul without Charlene, the ISK librarian. When I thought the boiler had exploded directly beneath her, I did not express to her my flood of feelings upon my relief in finding her safe, as I wasn't sure how she would respond. Up until this point in our time together, her silent ways had always left me guessing as to how she felt about me. However, communication was not her problem, for she often spoke with full assurance and clarity about topics she was passionate about and the expectations she had of others.

Our first encounter at our Pre-Field Orientation (PFO) in June 2005 birthed my insecurity about how she would respond to a newbie principal at ISK, or really anyone on the team.

"I work better alone. I consider that a strength."

I will never forget those first comments from Charlene when we met as new staff that summer. We had all completed our Myers-Brigg assessments and without Byron present for most of PFO, I led everyone in the group to share their personality descriptors around the circle. Her remarks hung unchallenged in the silent room. All eyes focused on the matronly black woman speaking firmly and without hesitation or even a smile.

Work better alone? You must be kidding, lady! How will this type of attitude work on a closed communal campus? Are we headed for problems, you and I? My thoughts raced around my mind, worrying about the impact of her big personality in our small spaces.

My next connection with Charlene was in the Dubai airport at the end of July as several ISK staff traveled together into Kabul. When the team learned at PFO that Michael and I had navigated this unique and confusing trek into Afghanistan before, many asked to join us in Dubai for the last leg of the journey.

"Over here, Charlene." Michael motioned to the woman in a bright orange tunic pantsuit with matching headscarf trudging our direction. She looked like she might be heading to Africa with her colorful outfit and pillows and large suitcases. He helped gather her belongings to the line where we waited to board the shuttle bus from Dubai Terminal One to Terminal Two where the smaller airlines serviced less popular, more remote locations. Places like Kabul, Afghanistan;

Peshawar, Pakistan; Tehran, Iran; and other cities I didn't even recognize.

I could tell Charlene was tired by how slowly she was moving along. We all were exhausted from the extended international travel. She found a seat and plopped down, letting Michael handle her collection alone.

"Are you okay?" I asked, not sure what else to say as I helped Michael pile up her supply of personal items.

"I will be fine." Not meeting my eyes, she fanned herself and dabbed at the sweat resulting from our less-than-air-conditioned waiting area.

Michael loaded an extra cart with her carry-ons that I would have to push for her since she already had one to navigate. I returned to my place in line with Michael and our kids and friends, and we exchanged glances. Anna gave me her arched-one-eyebrow look that I understood completely without words. In the sleep-deprived, overheated state I was in, critical thoughts flooded my mind.

I'm not sure if I will like this lady. She isn't going to survive Afghanistan with such an independent demeanor if she can't even handle her luggage by herself!

I knew I was in danger of creating a full negative profile of Charlene and twisting her every action to bolster my negative impression of her. I know not to do that to people; I am a trained counselor for heaven's sake, but she was just that strong in her word choice and facial expressions. I fluctuated between irritation, intimidation, and curiosity about her from the beginning.

"I am here to set up the library. It will take me several months to get things ordered and prepared. You need to find someone to help me with my teaching load so I can do what I need to do." Charlene delivered this message to me and Byron via email in the first weeks of ISK while she was in her second-grade classroom next door to the admin building. Communicating digitally rather than in person was easier on her body with our two-and-three story buildings spread over campus, plus her dust allergies and breathing issues.

"Get her what she wants, Gail. That's why Oasis hired her. We're lucky to have an experienced librarian here to set things up right." Byron reviewed the email and nodded in agreement. He figured out how to work amicably with Charlene early on, a strong personality himself.

"Where am I going to find a professional educator who can teach in English to elementary students who may not even know English? And do that part-time? And here in Kabul?" I stood staring at Byron, feeling frustrated at Charlene for the seemingly impossible situation she was demanding of me. He shrugged his shoulders, returned to his computer screen, and I left his office in a huff.

I did miraculously find a co-teacher for Charlene. Soon we began to spend more time together as she began creating the ISK library from nothing, no shelves, no books, and no computer system for cataloging or keeping track of inventory.

"No, that won't work, Gail. Here is what I need."

I heard such remarks from Charlene often. With our strong personalities and similar height, Charlene and I figuratively and literally stood eye-to-eye on many occasions. She demonstrated respect for me as her supervisor, but she made me earn it. I had to persuade her to follow my leadership at times in the early years—always in private conversations—but I determined to win her over to my viewpoint when necessary.

"How is it going with your librarian, Mom?" Anna asked

me on the phone several weeks after she was back in Missouri. "She is quite the personality, isn't she? Think you two will get along?"

"You know what? I do. I'm not sure we'll be friends, but that's not necessary if we can work well together, right?" I filled Anna in on the progress of the library and the activities of the other staff she had met in her short visit to ISK.

I got my answer soon enough about potential closeness with Charlene. I became agitated with her that first fall after the mortar blast when I perceived she was manipulating my generous, soft-hearted husband. ISK staff was provided cell phones with monthly allotments as part of our contract. Phoning our families back in the U.S. was therefore cheap, and we chatted often. Still, Michael and I tended to carry a balance of unused calling units month to month. Charlene somehow found this out.

"Mike, I need to borrow your phone, please. I'm out of units." I watched him hand his phone over to her and walk inside our apartment to give her privacy to make her call.

"Why did you do that, give her your phone?" I saw the courtyard exchange from our kitchen window. "I cannot believe how bold that woman is. Don't you think it's rude for her to expect you to share your minutes just because she used hers up?" Michael just shrugged his shoulders and let it slide.

The phone request came several more times from Charlene.

I could not let it go. After work one day while walking back to our lodgings from the admin building, I told her what I thought about the phone-borrowing situation.

"Well, it isn't really your business, is it?" she said dismissively and slowly climbed the steps to the Marble Mansion.

I stormed into my apartment and slammed the door within her earshot.

Michael challenged me later while eating dinner. "Let it go. We have plenty of phone units to meet our needs. Do you really want to pick a fight with her?"

Early on, he kept his space from Charlene, like many people. He was not afraid of her but was not drawn to her style of direct-opinionated conversation either.

In my mind, the issue was her boldness—not about whether we had enough units to spare.

"It isn't right." I put down my fork, no longer hungry. "What if every staff person asked us for this same favor, how could we pick and choose fairly?" My sense of justice was in overdrive. I remained upset into the evening.

Hours later, while sitting upstairs in our apartment reading and trying to think about something else besides the phone-borrowing issue, I heard a knock at the back door. As I went down the stairs, I heard my name called.

"Gail, could you come outside for a minute, please?" It was Charlene. I joined her on the courtyard, just a step from my apartment door. Her large brown eyes were moist, and a tortured look replaced her usual serene expression. "I need to ask your forgiveness. God has been correcting me since we spoke earlier. I was wrong to take advantage of Mike's giving nature, and I knew it. I don't want this between us. Can you forgive me?"

I watched her tears fall. I was stunned and moved.

The affection that had overwhelmed me a few weeks earlier when I thought she had been killed the night of the mortar blast returned in full measure. "Of course, I forgive you!" I gave her a hug and felt my judgments melt away. She hugged me back, blew her nose, nodded her head, and went back to her bedroom.

We never spoke of the incident again, but our relationship became cemented in mutual care and respect from that point forward. The truth of the matter was, she'd needed more monthly units to connect with booksellers for building the library, not just chatting with friends. We corrected the problem and increased her allotment.

I slowly realized that I really liked Charlene. I felt I understood her—most of the time. She had been on her own for several decades and did not leave her fate up to others if she had a preference, which she almost always did. After any discussions with me where I held my ground, she would press her lips together, nod her head, and get busy fulfilling her responsibilities without complaint or pushback, even if she still disagreed. She never went public with her grievances. I had to admire her maturity when not getting what she wanted.

Please come to the Marble Mansion. I need you to do something for me.

I read Charlene's text and wondered, *What now?* But I obediently stopped at her bedroom door before going to my apartment after school. But not with irritation and nervousness, we were past that by then. Time spent together, shared values, and the unique cross-cultural experience tended to bond global workers in Kabul. I felt that bond with Charlene.

"What's up?" I set my briefcase on her bed and joined her at her computer desk.

"I just got this email message. I need two cars and drivers tomorrow morning, first thing. My contact at the military base has received a partial shipment of library books, and they must be picked up ASAP. The cartons are too big to store for any time at the base's tiny post office. Can you arrange that? I need to go along to check that everything is in order so you will need to sub me out." Charlene was beaming. Her dream project was becoming a reality.

I nodded and gave her a high-five in celebration.

Charlene knew library book shipping would be free if we acquired a U.S. postal address in Kabul, saving thousands of dollars to buy more books. Using those same bold behaviors that had caused our phone-feud, Charlene had visited the military bases in Kabul until she figured out how to make the deliveries happen by recruiting cooperative U.S. service personnel. Deployed personnel changed quickly in Afghanistan, but Charlene stayed diligent developing new friendships on the bases for our important APO addresses.

Soon, an impressive collection of books began to stack up in the designated library space in the admin building near my office.

"They are all in perfect order to take right out and place on the shelves. When we unbox them, I will scan their ISBN code and all the pertinent information will automatically be in the ISK system, ready for check-out."

Byron and I were looking at the twenty plus numbered cartons and nodding appreciatively at the beginnings of the first-ever ISK library, while listening to Charlene explain how it all went together. This lady knew what she was doing, absolutely.

"Come see the shelves." Charlene said this to me in the fall of ISK's second year, not via email, but in person as she walked by my office to the library. A local Afghan carpenter had made the custom-sized shelving to fit into the only available, though still inadequate, library space. Coveted heating and air conditioning units were later installed to reduce wear and tear on the books and keep air circulating in the smallish library. Great for the books, studying students, and the librarian, too.

"How many volumes again? Four thousand?" I asked Charlene as I prepared for a tour by USAID folks to showcase the finished ISK trophy library. The array of beautiful, diverse, and dust-resistant hardcover books was the largest collection of English books in the country. Charlene ordered colorful, kid-friendly rugs and inspiring wall decorations for final touches. None of our early years' decision-making squabbles mattered in the face of what she accomplished with that library. It was magnificent and I was proud to be a part of the achievement with her.

Charlene came to me one day after the library was well established. Her schedule had become predictable in serving elementary classes weekly and allowing secondary English teachers access with their students during instruction time. She had also begun keeping students during lunch when they misbehaved during their library time.

"Let your teachers know they can send students to me to complete make-up work or serve discipline time for behavior issues. That way they can have their lunch break free." The offer was well received as teachers knew students did not want to be in trouble with Miss Crump. She carried a useful fear-factor, even though she was not harsh or punitive in her manner with students. They just knew she wouldn't put up with foolishness. Charlene could get the outcomes teachers wanted with difficult students, along with a hug as they left the library, go figure. She was a generous and caring team member and educator—once you got to know her.

"I need a good Western. Whatcha got?" Charlene texted me one weekend night. She proved interesting company outside of work. We began to share DVDs in the evenings with our similar tastes for gritty drama shows and would sometimes go out to Kabul restaurants together with Michael.

As the years continued to pass, Charlene remained at ISK as other team members came and went. Only a handful of staff could tell the early days' stories, and she and I truly knew the joys and agonies of establishing and growing the school from scratch. We were in each other's stories and memory books—and more importantly, we'd worked our way into each other's hearts.

"Hey. Let's go to Israel on fall break. Mandy has been there a few times and can be our tour guide to make use of the six days we'll have in-country." Charlene pitched the idea to Michael and me upon returning to Kabul in August 2010. Mandy was our high school English teacher who had lived on an Israeli kibbutz prior to coming to ISK. Charlene made her preferences for the trip known, but then so did we. The relational comfort level was well established, and the four of us covered much of Israel as Michael drove the rental car in accordance with Mandy's directions.

One night in Jerusalem, Charlene offered to pay for us to have dinner at the acclaimed King David Hotel restaurant. Michael could not refuse, although he would not have selected the pricey place on his own. The food was delicious, from the kosher gourmet mushroom soup appetizer to the well-prepared entrees and amazing desserts. The linen tablecloths and polished silverware plus scenic views overlooking the night-lit city from the hotel's high vantage point made for an elegant atmosphere. Everything felt wonderful, so relaxing.

But all of a sudden, our peace was hijacked.

"Do you hear that?" I whispered to Charlene. The woman at the table next to us, apparently intoxicated, began throwing up violently—actions that certainly did not fit the luxurious setting. Charlene and I began to giggle at how quickly we were brought out of our fanciful moment to real life, finally we ended up covering our mouths with our napkins in a vain attempt to silence ourselves.

Michael was not amused at our school-girl silliness and remained dignified, as we probably ought to have been.

But laughter is good therapy, and we laughed often together as we shared each other's lives more every year.

Michael and I traveled to Beijing with Charlene in November 2011. The China trip was full of precious memories like visiting the Great Wall, the Forbidden City, the pandas at the Beijing Zoo, an almost fatal bicycle-taxi ride, and an impressive Chinese Acrobat show. The three of us knew that it would be the finale of our time together in Kabul. Now house-mates in our fourth campus location over the years, Charlene knew about my upcoming departure in June 2012. It was time to leave Afghanistan after seven years to be grandma to my first granddaughter born three years earlier and a second one due in May.

Plus, my relationship with the ISK director was not going well. Byron had left in June 2009, and my new boss was completely different, and not in a good way for me. Without saying so, I could tell Charlene determined to make this week-long vacation a respite, a time of calm, and special memories. I was uncharacteristically stressed, and she knew me well enough to recognize it.

One evening near the end of our week, she and I sat in the hotel lounge, sampling appetizers and waiting for Michael to join us to leave for dinner. I told Charlene that he was planning to push for a McDonald's hamburger. We had eaten several local fare meals by this time, and we would not have the familiar fast-food option back in Kabul. My husband equates hamburgers with the best of American culture, along with salsa and tortilla chips. He also appreciates the relative cheapness of hamburgers.

"Forget McDonald's," Charlene said to me. "Let's stay in tonight, and Mike can get a burger here." Our international hotel had Asian as well as Western fare options on their restaurant menus.

I knew he would not want to pay the hotel price for a burger, but I wanted to stay put, also. I did not want to go back out into the Beijing crowds and lingering air pollution after our long day of sightseeing.

"I will pay for it. He will agree," she said with her usual confidence.

I sat back to watch the exchange as Michael appeared in the lounge area.

"Hey, Michael, listen. I don't want to go back out tonight. Let's eat here. My treat," she said in her typical direct manner. Michael looked at me. I said nothing. When I didn't speak up to confirm his earlier plan, he sighed and sat down.

"Okay, if that makes you girls happy," he responded. He looked at a menu, ordered his burger, and mentioned the outrageous price as I knew he would. Charlene waved away his concerns and settled back for deep conversation.

The burger may not have been worth fifteen dollars, but that evening became a treasure. For the first time during our trip, I began to express my anxiety about the upcoming ISK conflict with my boss. Charlene said little, letting me vent. I recognized compassion in her soft brown eyes. I felt her loyalty and support even though her comments were brief. The China burger therapy session helped me feel less alone in my trouble. I was grateful for her understanding without quips or easy advice.

A lot had happened in our relationship since that first meeting when she declared her desire for solitude. We both worked to develop a precious, mutually beneficial relationship. She was able to respond appropriately to my position of authority, yet allowed me to be myself in the off hours without awkwardness in the vertical-horizontal relational transitions. What if my original book cover type pre-judgments and negative assessments had stayed in place? I would have missed a generous gift God provided me throughout my Kabul years, a quality companion to fill the void of friendships left behind, and someone mature enough to navigate hanging out with the boss lady.

We've hosted Charlene back in the United States a couple of times already and I fully expect to see her in the future. Always carrying around books loaded on her Nook or one in her bag like the librarian lady she has always been, she is a low maintenance guest who enjoys a quality meal and feet-up, lengthy conversation. Our shared experience in Kabul created a strong bond; and I'm thankful I chose to engage in Charlene's story more deeply, not stopping with first impressions in order to discover the friend I needed.

The Unveiled Truth: As a coach, counselor, and educator, I know the dangers of pre-judging people. But as an imperfect human, I can fall into that trap just as easily as anyone else. My journey into a lasting relationship with Charlene proved to me, yet again, I need to chill out and get better acquainted, ask questions, and learn about someone before dismissing him or her from my *book* collection.

God knows who we need for specific challenging times of

our life, so we need to open our hearts and minds to His wisdom in the friendship selection process.

Take time to carefully read the human *books* He sends your way.

Who in your sphere confuses or even irritates you that deserves another read?

13

No Place to Hide

I remember the first time I emailed my friends back home about living and working on a closed compound with the people I supervised saying, "This scenario gives new meaning to the concept of *transparent leadership*."

Add living and working with my husband on a closed compound...

In the first few months of our arrival, while Michael fulfilled his commitment to work at ISK as the Operations Manager and I learned my principal role, we carried our leadership strain and stress everywhere we went. There was little privacy anywhere at any time for anyone, let alone for married couples.

With twenty-seven years of marriage under our belts, including the survival of some rough times during Michael's seminary days, we handled things in our own way. We moved freely in our ability to be *assertive* in our discussions. However, the other team members, especially the younger ones, apparently got nervous whenever our public conversations got heated.

During an admin team meeting after ISK had finally opened, I voiced my opinion over how to handle national workers on campus. There were several school projects still in process with winter coming. Afghanistan culture is soft on time, unlike Westerners with our expectations for immediate results. To me and many of the staff, our workers seemed frustratingly slow to accomplish tasks. But not to my husband, their supervisor.

"We really need Building C finished. I have two groups on top of each other in Building D and music classes still using the basement of the Marble Mansion, which is supposed to be staff space only." I knew my tone was not great, but I felt the pressure of unhappy students and teachers weighing on me.

All eyes looked at Michael.

"The cement on the second floor of Building C is not drying quickly so I have the men doing other tasks while waiting. You'll just have to tell your teachers to be patient." Michael looked in my direction briefly and then handed Byron the receipt for a new generator.

"Well, when I see your guys standing around, it looks like nothing is happening. I can't give a good explanation for that to a teacher with fifteen students crowded into a closet-sized room." I directed my comments to Byron, but clearly I was responding to my husband.

"So since you don't really know what the guys are working on, you can't really judge what they are accomplishing, can you? This is not the U.S. Everything takes longer." Michael gestured emphatically showing his irritation with my continued pressing.

Neither of us acted like there were five other people in the room.

"Okay, so we're done here. Thanks, folks." Byron stood up and then asked me, "Could you and Michael stay a minute?" We remained in our seats as the others left and he closed the door.

"Now, being that I'm separated from my wife, I'm probably the last person who should give out marital advice." He moved to a chair closer to us. "And I realize times are stressful for both of you, but this thing you guys are doing..." He made a circling motion with his hand toward us. "Well, you're scaring the kids!"

Michael and I exchanged surprised looks. *This thing? The kids?* (We referred to the rest of the staff who were much younger than Byron, Michael, and I endearingly as "the kids.")

Almost in unison, we shot back, "What do you mean? How are we scaring anybody?"

Byron rested his arms on his chair and waited silently to let the answer come to us.

Oh. The arguing, interrupting, bickering, fussing...

Separating work from home was difficult, considering our apartment was literally a two-minute walk from the office. Not treating each other well, especially in public where young adults (a.k.a. *the kids*) were observing, made them uncomfortable and worried that our marriage was in trouble—or worse, that this was what a long-time relationship sinks into over time and under stress.

We both took a deep, resigned breath and looked at each other, minus the eye-daggers from before.

"Byron, we are sorry." Michael took my hand. "You're right. We need to behave better. This is the first time we have ever worked at the same place in all our married life. I'm from the business world where customer service is the focus."

"And I've worked in schools my whole career, so bells and clocks are my constant motivator, while Michael is all about people and not so time-oriented. That's perfect for Afghan culture and relationship building, but not so much for school needs." I lifted embarrassed eyes to my boss to check for understanding. "Seems we're struggling to figure out how to work together."

Byron nodded. "I get it. I think you guys are great, and I couldn't be happier to have you here with me since you're both excellent at serving the needs of others, but how about taking some time for yourselves? Are we good?"

Master of the short meeting, Byron stood to signal we were done. He gave us each a brotherly hug before opening the door, where a line of people waited to question each of us.

Michael and I paid more attention to our behavior and the tone of our conversations after that, often taking dinner to our apartment to have daily debriefing time away from the oh, so public audience. We also tried to get off campus to local restaurants or coffee shops periodically, even when the workload weighed heavily on our leader-shoulders and called our names twenty-four seven.

After his first year as ISK campus facilities manager, Michael changed jobs to teaching adult English classes and leadership training for Afghan managers, government officials, and military and business leaders. This gave us some appreciated work-space.

As constant proximity breeds familiarity, I found the lines between boss and campus teammate difficult to separate as well. Byron lived in a separate building at the end of our street and rarely took his meals in the dining hall. I thought this was not the best approach, at least not for me, and Michael felt the same way. We tried to get counsel and insight from other international leaders in Kabul on how to approach living with our staff so near, but most allowed their team to live in their own homes or apartments around town, so not quite the same scenario.

I never felt I kept the line between boss and friend perfectly defined. In the early years, as a nervous new school leader, I struggled to switch out of job mode. I made lots of mistakes and hurt my relationships with staff, who I wanted nothing more than to encourage and support. An example happened in the second year.

Six days each week, Sakhi prepared lunch and dinner for the team and served it in our common dining room. We were permitted to take food to another location, but most people just popped in, ate, chatted with whoever was present at the time, and then went on to their classroom or apartment.

One night at dinner, coming straight from my office across the street, I entered the line to fill a plate. I heard a table of secondary teachers laughing and reviewing bits of the day. Finding high schoolers typically unfunny, I was intrigued to discover the topic which was being shared so publicly.

"So, there is Arif big as life with a t-shirt sporting a huge cannabis leaf with a smoking reefer at the bottom. It was all done in various shades of green, so I had to look twice to be sure I was seeing what I thought I was seeing." The science teacher was seated in the middle of the table surrounded by other staff.

"I saw that! He acted pretty proud of his new American shirt. I wondered if he understood the *Homegrown Happiness* message. His English is not great." Another teacher added as the group at the table chuckled.

When I heard the third and fourth teacher exclaim, "Oh, yeah, I saw that too!" I couldn't take it anymore. I walked over with my full plate and said, "Let me get this straight. All of you saw the offensive shirt and nobody did anything about it?"

Silence at the table. Silence in the whole dining room. All eyes on me.

I knew my face was flushed and my expression intense. Out of the corner of my eye, I saw Michael motion me over to where he was sitting with a few other, older staff members. I quickly went and sat down. People began to clear out of the dining room. Michael made small talk with our table companions while I moved the food around my plate. After a few minutes, I dropped my utensils in the kitchen and went to our apartment.

Michael joined me in our upstairs sitting area a bit later where I was staring out the window at the Kabul mountains. He was quiet at first, wise man that he is. Finally, he gently broke the tension by asking, "Do you think you should have reprimanded them at dinner with everyone watching?"

I sighed. "No, I'm sure I shouldn't have done that. It's just so hard when you hear things like that and you are the stinking school leader! When can I feel I am 'off-duty' like they obviously do?"

He put his arm around me on our small loveseat and said nothing more. He recognized that having nowhere to vent at ISK with neutral parties heightened the stress levels for everyone. He understood as well as anyone that leadership issues are often complicated, but this situation was particularly challenging.

"What should I do to fix this?" I sat in a pouty posture in front of Byron the day after the drug-shirt incident. "Why didn't those teachers do anything about the situation? Our handbook is clear on wearing shirts with war/drug/violence/profanity themes." I folded my arms tight across my chest, shaking my head in disbelief.

"Okay, they messed up, obviously. But if they had their own homes across town, you wouldn't have heard this conversation. So where do they go to debrief and vent their workday? They are caught just like we are with little privacy." Byron paced his office while glancing out his second story window at the PE class in the courtyard below.

He finally sat down across from me, but not behind his desk. "What do you want to do?"

"I can't do nothing. I know that. We all live together, for goodness' sake!" After a couple of minutes, I said with as much confidence as I could muster, "I'll go to each one and apologize for embarrassing them publicly. And I'll try my best not to excuse my behavior by bringing up their failings which hacked me off in the first place. How is that?"

Byron nodded and returned to his computer. "Let me know how it goes. I got your back."

As I walked toward the high school building, thoughts flooded my overwrought head and heart.

I wish I had someplace to go, to get away from everyone and everything. Man, I feel trapped and, yes, mad. And homesick. And like I'm not doing such a great job. Help me, God. You brought me here.

I could feel my inner turmoil lessening with the apology plan, although I also knew I needed to let go of pride. This was seriously humbling stuff I was about to do. My stomach knotted.

"Do you have a minute?" I approached the first apology recipient on his way to lunch, but presently alone on the walkway. "I am so sorry for my reaction at dinner last night. That was wrong on so many levels. I hope you can forgive me. I have a lot to learn about being a quality principal and team leader."

"Yeah, that was tough. No problem. I should've dealt with the t-shirt. I forget about the dress code since my former school didn't enforce one. We're good, thanks for talking to me." He looked right at me and shook my hand with a smile. "It means a lot."

Whew. One down, three to go.

The other conversations went about the same, I owned my mistake and they recognized they needed to up their game as school rules' gatekeepers. I felt exhausted and gave myself permission to go home early that day after all the apologies were made.

When I told Karen I was leaving before school was out, she discreetly said with concern in her eyes, "It'll be fine. Don't worry about it."

Of course Karen knew how I'd messed up so publicly, everyone in our little ISK universe knew everyone's business.

That afternoon, I distracted myself with a gripping mystery movie at home with the curtains closed. I made myself a batch of buttered popcorn and had not one, but two Diet Cokes to further pamper myself.

By the time dinner came around, only twenty-four hours after the principal-fail, I was doing okay. I joined Michael in the dining hall that night with my head up and a tired, but sincere smile positioned on my face. The atmosphere was a bit awkward, but staff members smiled back at me.

The challenge to know when to remove the principal hat for me was occasionally flipped. Sometimes staff forgot I was actually wearing one, and they needed to remember who was at the top of our vertical relationship.

One day after a staff movie night in the Marble Mansion, I

called one of the teachers into a meeting with Byron and me about an upcoming school-wide, public event. At one point in the discussion, as we outlined our expectations, she told us both, "No, there's not enough time to do this to my standards."

We tried to explain our reasons for the event and how it would help parents understand our balanced arts curriculum, but her face grew tighter and redder as we spoke. "Maybe in a few months, but I don't want to do it now. You can't make me if I say I'm uncomfortable."

I looked at Byron to see if he felt the same incredulity I did. It appeared this *young* employee forgot to whom she was talking. *You can't make me? Did she really say that?*

"Well, actually, we can require you to do this. Then afterward, you can decide if you still want to work at ISK." Byron calmly but firmly set the record straight, not taking his eyes from the teacher.

I didn't know what to say, so I just watched.

The teacher cried. I followed Byron's lead to sit in silence. Then as reason returned, she looked up and made an enlightening comment. "I'm sorry I reacted this way. But it's hard to go from lounging together over popcorn and videos like friends to taking orders! I sometimes forget you are my bosses."

All three of us laughed and nodded in agreement. What a crazy set-up to live and work in.

She put together a stellar, short notice, no frills event and showcased our students with excellence, just as we thought she would. The parents stopped asking me to take their students out of music and art and other extra-curricular subjects that would develop brainpower, creativity, and character after they saw the results of such instruction during the program.

Off ISK campus (after a couple of years struggling to live

two separate lives in one tiny bubble), God provided a special gift for me to be fully transparent about my challenges and needs as ISK's principal. I was invited to participate in a monthly prayer meeting for international NGO group leaders in Kabul. We met early before work at the facilitator's home and placed our cell phones in a room far from the gathering for security and privacy.

With a hot cup of tea and sometimes breakfast, the group sat in a circle of chairs. In divisions of three, we each had the chance to share as personally as desired. Then the total group would pray for the three and move around the circle in like fashion. Only one person from each organization was present, intentionally, to afford the leaders freedom to share their struggles with personnel, Afghan government, finances, health, family, or whatever weighed down their hearts.

Most of the group were men, but I felt affirmed and respected for the tough job I had running a top-quality school in Afghanistan. A few times, I wept as I shared, allowing myself to release stored-up emotions over my hurts and disappointments in the freeing absence of ISK people. Along with sympathy, I received empathy since the others endured similar problems with younger staff wanting more liberty and the national staff issues we all faced. I appreciated this monthly respite and learned much from my fellow leaders.

For seven years I lived in this glass house ISK setting, learning to do the very thing I often advised my former public-schooled students who ended up at ISK. When they complained that the small school environment gave people access to everybody's business, I told them: "Make peace with living in the light. Stay out of trouble and you'll be fine."

I knew more about what I was preaching than those students could appreciate. I had no place to hide in my own current life at home or at school, so I needed to behave my best at all times.

But really, shouldn't we always do so?

The Unveiled Truth: I try to help my clients close the gap between their *public* and *private* self as much as possible. This takes honest reflection, correction of bad motivations and actions, and intention to do better.

Cultivating humility and humor in our lives helps narrow the gap. Finding a caring community to give supportive feedback and celebrate success is also key to our personal growth.

It is only natural to act your best in public and let your worst come out at home. But when home is just about as public as the workplace, like my ISK situation, the challenge is to monitor behavior at all times. This is tough, but not impossible.

Don't let the stress of your public work life make a mess of your relationships at home.

Who needs better behavior from you, some more consideration, and perhaps a request for their forgiveness...today?

14

The Power to Change Comes from Within

When I first arrived in Kabul, I decided to study Dari so I could communicate on some level with the local people. I was an educator committed to lifelong learning after all. Many of the ISK staff also wanted language lessons.

The two former KIA teachers joining ISK introduced us to Aqilla. She had years of experience teaching Dari to foreigners and could bridge the gap with her own accumulation of English. Several of us began classes in August 2005 with Aqilla before ISK opened, and we planned to continue learning in the late afternoons during the school term. It was hard work focusing on the intricacies of the Persian language and the wiggly-worm Arabic script.

During our vision-casting sessions in August, I had the revelation along with Byron that we needed to add some cultural instruction to our diverse student body.

"What do you think about hiring Aqilla to teach Dari to ISK students and weave in some Afghan history and traditions? I would hate for international students to attend our American school right here in Kabul and leave without any native culture or language learning. Wouldn't you?" I threw out my ideas to Byron while standing in one of the unfinished classroom buildings taking notes on the work still needed.

"How would we do it? Where would we put her classes?" He brainstormed strategies as we moved to the next building to inventory progress. "Plus, we have such a mix of students, native speakers, complete novices, and expat kids who have already picked up Dari from their years living in Pakistan among the Afghan refugees. That's a wide range of abilities."

"Let me talk with her and see what her thoughts are. I'll get back to you." I returned to my office to call Aqilla, and Byron left to visit with Michael about the checklist we'd developed for the workers. I had learned my lesson on who was best at work-related conversations with my conscientious husband. (Not me.)

Aqilla came that afternoon to my office. "Yes, Mrs. Goolsby, how may I help you?" She waited until I gestured for her to sit down and I joined her from around my desk.

She listened without interruption to my thoughts about her joining the ISK staff part-time to teach Dari to our students and bring aspects of Afghanistan inside the American school walls. When she leaned forward or looked quizzical, I rephrased, remembering to speak slowly and with carefully chosen words, not using casual American vocabulary.

"I understand you have been a teacher for many years in Afghan schools. So you have teaching credentials, correct? Tell me more about your experiences and what you think of our idea." I finished my part of the conversation and sat back to listen as carefully as I had tried to communicate.

"This is a very great honor. I do not know if my years as a biology teacher in Afghan schools will be enough for ISK. But if you will help me learn new methods for teaching, I am ready to do my best." She took the teacup I offered her from the tray on my desk and told me more about her educational training.

At one point, Aqilla grew thoughtful. "Mrs. Goolsby, this is important for Afghan students as well as foreign students. Many do not know their own language, and this is not good. So many have lived outside Afghanistan as refugees or to escape war. Maybe they speak Dari, but not read or write it. I feel they must learn their own tongue."

Days later, I officially hired her to teach Dari part-time and to include Afghan cultural lessons. Both of us were excited at the new knowledge we were adding to the curriculum.

However, Aqilla's heart to share about her beloved Afghanistan to her own country's children proved to be the hardest part of our plan.

My naïvety about Afghanistan's power-posture culture exploded in my face. I had never imagined Aqilla would be treated differently than any other ISK instructor.

From the first announcement of the Dari requirement, I had to explain and defend the decision to our Afghan parents who only wanted more English, science, and math. Byron and I stood our ground, not realizing that this decision would actually work in our favor in the months ahead with the cranky Ministry of Education (MOE). Not long after we hired Aqilla, the MOE declared ISK needed to teach the same courses as Afghan schools, including Dari.

But our Afghan students—following their parents' lead—from the privileged ones to the less affluent, disrespected Aqilla time and time again. Like spoiled, entitled children, they felt somehow superior to her, like she worked for them. She did not complain, and I remained unaware of the Dari mutiny until some whistleblowers came to my office a few weeks into the semester.

"Mrs. Goolsby, can we enter?" The two female high school students came to my office doorway at lunchtime.

I looked up from my computer screen, making note of their serious faces. They came close to my desk and in low voices described the injustice happening daily to Aqilla.

"The boys are awful to Mrs. Khalq. Even some of the girls. It isn't right. They talk when she is teaching and get out of their seats no matter what she says. We feel badly for her and wanted to tell you. But please don't say it was us." Big brown eyes stared at me, waiting for my reply.

I stood to give them reassuring hugs. "Thank you, ladies. I will take care of it. And I will not mention how I came to know this information, so don't worry."

Instead of going to find Byron, I knew my best help would be my culture expert, Khalid. He had the perfect combination of Afghan insight as well as embracing the standards at ISK. His own quality family upbringing would not have allowed such disrespect either.

"I am going to stand outside the door of the Dari classroom and listen, but I will not understand what they are saying. Will you come with me?" I had barely finished explaining the problem when Khalid popped up from his chair and started for the door almost ahead of me. I could see he was angry at the situation.

"I will be as Columbo," he whispered as we headed down

to the building where Aqilla held her afternoon classes. "I will gather evidence and trap them in their own game."

We selected the class with the oldest Afghan students in the school. After the bell rang and the door was closed, we moved to stand silently in the hallway. It was easy to identify the troublemakers, the mature male voices were loud and frequent, and Aqilla's a poor match. The laughing and obvious movement of bodies told us the truth of what was going on, and it wasn't orderly learning.

Khalid's eyes burned with indignation. We slipped out of the building before the class was over and found Byron to report the trouble in detail. His tight jaw and hand smack on the desktop communicated that his feelings mirrored ours. The combined counsel was for me to handle this, as a woman and the leader in charge of hiring staff for ISK, starting with a conversation with Aqilla.

"I've come to understand what is happening, Aqilla, with your Dari classes. I am very disappointed in the ISK students."

She quickly looked down to her lap as she realized why I had brought her into my office after school. "Please, Mrs. Goolsby, this is my responsibility. Do not be upset with the students. I will do a better job." She looked up and quickly added while twisting her headscarf, "I love the international students very much. They are so polite and trying their best."

"Khalid has helped me understand the prejudiced attitude these students have from their parents and Afghan traditions. However, in this school, we are teaching respect for all people, regardless of race, gender, religion, or nationality." I gently but firmly dismissed her plea to handle this alone and told her what would be taking place the next day. I could tell she was very nervous when she left my office.

During a loud, chaotic exchange in the high school Dari

class the next day, I opened the door unannounced. I stood silently for several minutes until like a rippled wave, students became aware of my presence and froze in place. It remains one of my strongest principal memories.

"Sit down and be quiet," I said in a calm, low voice.

Big male bodies found desks and slid in quickly and everyone sat up straight. A crowd of dark eyes stared at me, then looked down at their laps. They knew.

"Dr. Greene and I are very disappointed that students at ISK, the most prestigious school in Afghanistan, would treat one of our teachers this way. Now, I know Mrs. Khalq is not from America or England or Canada like other ISK teachers, but that is not the point." I moved up and down the crowded aisle to make eye contact with as many students who would look at me. I kept my face impassive, trying not to express as much emotion as I felt.

"I hired Mrs. Khalq. She is worthy of your respect as a professional educator, and I require you to respond to her just like your other teachers. Do you understand?" Male and female heads nodded, not all, but most. "If you have any questions about what I expect of you, please come to my office. In the meantime, please appreciate that you have the opportunity to be the best Dari speakers of your generation. This will prepare you to contribute to the future of Afghanistan."

I knew I was utilizing the powerful shame element of Afghan culture, but my message of acceptance and tolerance of different cultures was consistent with our weekly character assemblies and all ISK policies.

After this episode, most of the children modified their behavior and the parents began to recognize the benefit Mrs. Khalq provided their children. Her attendance numbers at parent-teacher conferences always beat the rest of the staff.

She knew almost every student in ISK since they had to meet the Dari requirement for graduation. The Afghan parents, struggling to speak English with Western teachers, felt she was approachable. Aqilla also made many personal calls to help struggling students and assisted fellow staffers with Afghan parent translation.

Even with these extra challenges, I never once regretted my choice to hire Aqilla. Part of the ISK vision to offer hope for Afghanistan's future leaders included raising their national/ethnic identity and increasing their language proficiency. I knew this effort was good and right, whether the students recognized it or not.

Despite the fact we never totally beat the ugly dynamic of disrespect from native students with Mrs. Khalq, or other national instructors we employed over the years, the children always knew where we stood. Our strict expectations allowed those students who wanted to embrace a higher way to behave to distance themselves from the mockers without too many negative repercussions from their peers.

But Aqilla had more than just disrespectful students to deal with, she faced another prejudice I could not help her with, the suspicion and judgment resulting from working for foreigners.

We discovered in our early years that Afghans who worked for foreigners often were shunned or hassled by relatives or neighbors. Aqilla never confessed this information to me, because of loyalty and gratitude most likely, but I often wondered. I knew her grown daughter who worked for USAID had secured private daily transportation to her job downtown because of the dangers she faced working for Americans.

"We are looking for a different house. Please pray for us." Aqilla shared this information one day in my office. This was not the first time she'd come to me as our bond grew stronger. I closed the door and sat close, holding her hands, praying for her large family's housing needs. She wiped her eyes and hugged me tightly before leaving to go home. The Khalq family moved a few times in our years together and I was not privy to all the reasons, but I worried over how much harassment she likely endured to serve us so well at ISK.

One of the projects that came to ISK depended on Aqilla's bi-lingual skills and educational knowledge. It pulled back the curtain of out-dated Afghan educational pedagogy and tradition—hard for me to hear about and hard for me to accept.

In 2008, ISK joined forces with another USAID project, the Partnership for Advancing Community Education in Afghanistan (PACE-A), to showcase the instruction of reading. We invited a handful of Afghan teacher trainers to observe our lower elementary teachers teach literacy for several days and then conducted a workshop using the methods they observed.

Aqilla was invaluable for this endeavor, along with our ISK Literacy Coach, who was a California educator, trained to work with ESL students, and an accomplished Dari speaker. I could tell Aqilla was proud of being a part of ISK and did more than translate when working with her national peer educators; she tried to convince them of these new methods for the good of all Afghan school children.

"Why do the teachers hug the students and greet them by name?" The Afghan administrators asked Aqilla the first day of ISK observation. "Why do they place some students close to them?"

With our help, Aqilla did her best to explain the importance of building relationships between teachers and students and recognizing the various learning needs of each one. Using the children's names in the lessons, displaying their quality work in the classroom, and assisting them to develop self-discipline by close proximity are simple yet impactful ways to help them learn.

One day during the PACE-A cooperative effort, Aqilla came to my office in tears. She was working so hard to help, what could have gone wrong? I sat at my desk and waited.

"When I am in the classrooms of small children with ISK teachers, I am broken-hearted. I am remembering my sweet little girl Ousay and the terrible pain she had attending school." Aqilla wiped her face with her headscarf and took the water bottle I offered her while continuing her sad story.

"She was just crying. She did not understand about going to school and being away from her mother. I watched as the teacher gave her a swat and told her to stop crying and take her seat. No caring words, no hug of comfort for my little girl, just harshness. This went on for days, and I cried the hours at home knowing she was crying at school. How I wish she had been given patient, loving teachers like here at ISK. It would have made all the difference."

I needed a tissue myself after that story. There was nothing to say. Nothing I could do to make it better for now grown-up Ousay or the thousands of Afghan children still enduring this type of school treatment.

Maybe we represented only a tiny drip in a vast dry cavern, but we believed ISK was making an impact. We both held our heads up proudly as we returned to the PACE-A workshop and tried to alter the old-fashioned thinking of the MOE teacher trainers.

My power as principal of ISK, the highest-level college-prep school in Afghanistan, had its limits for impacting change in our students, parents, staff, and surrounding culture. We planted seeds as thick as we could in every lesson, every classroom, every policy to teach respect and the worth of all people, but we were pushing against a mighty tide of default thinking and ingrained practices. I could not make anyone do anything; transformation was required from the inside.

Having staff like Aqilla and Khalid, along with Afghan families who stood for the same ideals as ISK, helped us know our hearts and instruction were in the right place. We did not have all the power needed to make robust, far-reaching changes in the country, but we used the platforms we had and gave it our all.

The Unveiled Truth: I learned about *positional power* in my leadership lessons and embraced the truth that *relational power* lasts much longer and has more of an effect. Person-to-person impact is worth the extra time.

Wanting to help is noble but not always feasible. It is right for us to try to use whatever resources we have available, but realism must have its place when it comes to influence and true power.

Utilize the relationships and open doors afforded you to share, affirm, challenge, and teach life lessons, so you can leave a positive mark that will last long after you are gone. Perhaps better ideas will be absorbed, and mindsets will truly be altered.

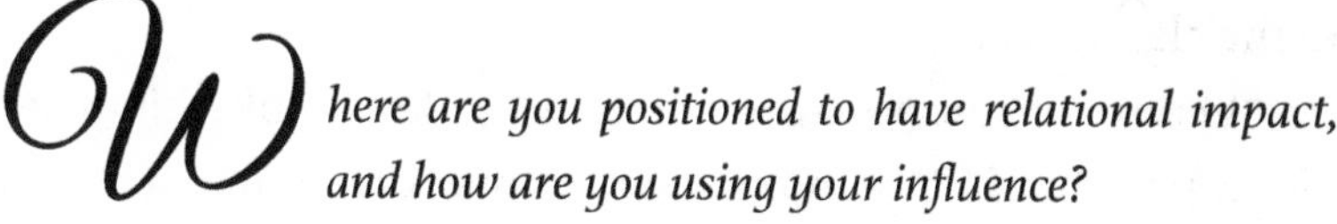

Where are you positioned to have relational impact, and how are you using your influence?

15

Try Something New

During my first two years, I was the only principal at ISK, so I handled all K-12 behavior issues. I was happy to later hire an assistant principal to help with young men in 7-12. The majority of ISK students were male, and because they are so valued in Asian families, they often are not told "no" until they come to school. Quite the set-up for teachers and administrators. Therefore, I spent the majority of my time dealing with boys over girls. This is not uncommon around the world.

As a former kindergarten teacher, I recognized little boy academic challenges and had a heart to help them assimilate while still enjoying all the energy and freshness they brought to the classroom.

"I can't get him to write his name or letters like his sister did in preschool," one mother said to me back in my Missouri classroom as she introduced me to her second-born. "I don't know how he will do in kindergarten." Her eyes searched mine for encouragement.

I smiled at this common confession by Western parents about their outdoor-oriented, big-motor driven boys (and some girls, too). "Don't worry. It will come together. Children do not get their teeth or walk at the same age either. He will learn to read and write in his time. Enjoy him for who he is."

In Afghanistan, younger children are often not exposed or expected to embrace academics before formal schooling begins, generally age seven. They venture outside the home compound rarely and only with the full family group. Operating traditional K4 and kindergarten classes with Afghan children unaccustomed to spending any length of time on their own was extremely challenging.

One little guy at ISK refused to accept he had to lie down for fifty minutes after lunch in the kindergarten classroom. With early morning rising a common Afghan practice, small bodies needed this quiet respite to make it through the afternoon. Little Mansur would not cooperate.

"Can you help me? I've tried everything I know, and Mansur is just not having it." The seasoned early childhood teacher spoke to me during recess while we watched her active charges. "Every other student is resting or sleeping fine, but not Mansur. He gets up and tries to play and even points to the door like he wants to go outside." She took a deep breath and threw up her arms in desperate surrender. "The other Pashto speaking students have told him the rest time rules, but he just laughs at them like it is a big joke."

"Well, I can try, though I'm not sure what I can do to add to your efforts. Mansur has complained about rest time to his mother and she wants me to put him in first grade so he doesn't have to lie down at all." I held up my hands to stop the teacher's protest forming on her face. "I know, I know. That is ridiculous and he is nowhere near ready for that. I asked Khalid to translate my answer on the phone to Mansur's mother the other day. He is staying in kindergarten, so we need to figure out how to get him on track."

I went to the kindergarten room the next day as we planned. I could hear the soothing instrumental music as I approached the door. When I opened it, I saw the darkened room and the large carpeted floor covered with little bodies under blankets, all still, some asleep, except one wriggly mass, Mansur.

As soon as he saw me, he sat up and began waving and blowing me kisses. I stopped with my hand on the doorknob.

Hmm. He thinks he's won. Skipping rest time to go to the principal's office would be like a prize. I need another plan.

I nodded to the teacher and closed the door. A new strategy came to me.

I went outside the building and spoke to three of our national workers in the maintenance office, all fathers and dedicated family men. Knowing that men often carry more impact than women regarding discipline, I explained the situation and asked for their help in talking to Mansur about following the rules for rest time. They agreed and followed me to the door of the kindergarten room.

I opened the door and motioned for Mansur to come with me. He hopped to the door and came dancing into the hall. I wish I had a video of his little face the moment it went from a charming, victorious smile to utter shock when he saw the three men standing there waiting for him.

The tallest and gentlest man of the crew bent down and took Mansur's small hand in his big one and spoke in Pashto all that I had requested, not raising his voice above a whisper.

Mansur's wide eyes never left the man's face, nodding a couple of times but remaining completely silent for this minute or two of instruction.

At the finish, Mansur looked up at me, nodded respectfully and went back into his classroom. He crawled onto his mat, pulled his blanket over his head, and promptly went to sleep.

Every single day following, he performed the same napping routine and never gave his teacher further resistance.

I have no idea what that man said, but that kind of father-back-up served me well the few times I needed it.

I had compassion for the young troublemakers, most just unfamiliar with school expectations. However, bigger students presented bigger challenges, and the most common visitors to my office were junior high boys.

One year, the secondary teachers calculated mathematically that whoever sat in close proximity to a particular seventh-grade male student would have a lower grade. Zahir was a poster child for ADHD and all the craziness of early adolescent boyhood. His smile and general happy demeanor made all of us like him in spite of his constant class distractions.

Zahir's teachers and I tried every method and management technique known to Western education professionals, including several conferences with the parents and an older sister (Afghan families often assign responsibilities for siblings to older children or relatives).

"He has not had these problems at his other schools," Zahir's dad stated this more than once to the circle of teachers I'd gathered together at the first conference.

I could tell by the looks silently exchanged between my staff that they did not believe his statement. But they knew as I did that Afghan teachers carry sticks and paddling boards to keep order. This is an accepted, and even an expected, way to discipline by Afghan school personnel. The same behavioral expectations and consequences often did not happen at home to these favored sons.

"Mr. Ahmadi, I am aware of how those schools handle misbehavior. We want Zahir to learn self-control to develop strong character and a good reputation. We will not be beating your son at ISK." I spoke slowly and calmly to Zahir's parents, allowing the older daughter time to translate to the mother, who sat with her headscarf over most of her face. I think she was crying or maybe just nervous to be seen in the presence of three male teachers.

A week later, the social studies teacher reported to me at lunch about Zahir's progress. "He did better for two or three days, but then his old ways resurfaced. We can't have productive discussions in class without his joking and interrupting. My geography class voted him off to the Siberian Gulag!"

I smiled at the international school version of time-out that the students had created as peer frustration mounted with Zahir's never-ending antics. He was sent to a corner of the classroom with PE mats blocking his view of the class. No audience to perform for. *Smart kids.*

Zahir was slow to comply with needed changes and teachers were pulling out their hair over his negative impact in their classrooms. I had to back up my staff's expectations for Zahir with strong action, so I determined to send him home for a week's suspension. Byron and the teachers supported my plan.

"This is not a permanent decision, I hope." I needed Khalid's superior translation talents to make sure the parents understood what suspension entailed as we met in my office. "Zahir must understand how serious this problem is. I want him to know if he hopes to remain a student at ISK, which is what we desire, things must change in his behavior."

More tears from the mother as they sat defeated in my office. Mr. Ahmadi seemed a kind, yet ineffective parent who loved his children but understood little how to train them. After I finished my instructions, Khalid spoke to the parents on his own, encouraging them to believe that Mrs. Goolsby knew best how to help their son.

I could only hope I knew what I was doing.

The older and middle sister came to my office every day during Zahir's suspension week, following parent directives, no doubt. I endured a play-by-play of the misery happening throughout their home. My hope that this plan would work lessened with each report.

"Our father locked Zahir in his room Thursday and Friday (the Afghan weekend) and only provided water and bread for him. Then Saturday and Sunday, while we were at school, Zahir was directed to sweep with a broom all day throughout the house."

I was taken aback at these drastic family decisions and punishments, but then again, they were trying to get their son's attention. Whatever worked was our collective goal.

"Please, Mrs. Goolsby, can Zahir return?" The sisters were waiting in the admin building foyer as I came to school on their brother's fourth out-of-school suspension day. "Our mother is crying all day and into the night. She is so afraid Zahir will not be allowed to come back to ISK. She believes his life is ruined." The girls came close to grasp my hand in their best pleading posture.

Such drama! I held my ground for the full five days of at-home suspension.

After brainstorming with Zahir's teachers, I remembered

the student-created Siberian exile. With my colleagues' agreement, I decided to bring him back on campus the next week for additional suspension in a selected area in a large basement room in the admin building. It was a storage area with high walls that did not reach the ceiling. No one could see him, but he would be supervised and accessible by staff members at all times. The family was incredibly grateful.

And no surprise, but after days of solitary sweeping and prisoner meals, Zahir was ecstatic to return to school! His sisters escorted him to Karen's desk, and she delivered him to his private classroom. The plan was for his teachers to send assignments and proctor quizzes and tests in their break time to catch him up in his classes.

The morning of his first in-school suspension day, I visited Zahir's assigned space two floors below my office.

"What is all this?" I burst out when entering his new domain. Zahir had decorated the walls with American ball caps on random hooks. Packs of M&Ms and Twix bars lay on book boxes throughout the storage space. "Where did all this candy come from?"

"Oh, please, Mrs. Goolsby, please have some." Zahir hopped up energetically and tried to press candy into my hand with a huge smile. "I brought it from home."

"Okay, Zahir, here's the thing. You're still in trouble, and this is not a party place. You need to focus on doing schoolwork. Remember our deal for you to earn your position back on campus?" I put the candy back down on the box.

He nodded humbly—and without adding more words, a change from earlier conversations with Zahir.

"Pack up the ball caps and candy and take them home. No more treats. You will be given time to get lunch and bring it back here to eat, but no other food, understood?" Again, more grateful agreement from my reforming student as he stuffed the offending articles away.

What a funny guy! I left quickly before he could hear me giggle over his private party decorations.

On the second day of Zahir's in-school suspension, I had a surprise visit from a well-dressed man I'd never met before. The school guards accompanied him to my office according to ISK procedure but stayed longer than usual.

I stood. And though I usually greeted a guest at the door, I stayed behind my desk.

"What can I do for you?" I asked.

The visitor reached into his suit coat pocket and offered his business card, saying in clear English, "I understand you are having some difficulties with Zahir Ahmadi."

I hesitated as I glanced at the card but gestured for him to sit. The name on the card was not familiar. "I am sorry, but I am not able to speak about a student without the parents' permission. How do you know Zahir?" I looked at the three-piece suit and tasteful shirt and tie ensemble.

"But of course. Zahir's mother is my sister. She requested that I meet with you to help with Zahir."

I remained silent, not knowing if the family connection was true or not.

He continued, "Please call me if you have any additional problems with Zahir. I am available at any time and will come to the school immediately at your request."

My curiosity burned. "If I call you, what happens?"

My visitor made a slight nod with his head, not looking directly at me, and said, "I will take care of the problem."

He said nothing else.

In a rare moment for me, I could not think of anything to say. Soon he stood, smiled, bowed slightly, and turned to go.

The guards escorted him off campus, and I immediately went downstairs to see Zahir.

"Hello, Mrs. Goolsby. How are you today?" Zahir spoke in his typical sunny manner and stood beside his desk at my entrance. (These traditional Afghan greetings for educators were well-loved by me and my ISK staff, although they disappeared once the students realized it was not required. Too bad.)

"I just had a very interesting visitor. He said he was your mother's brother and was sent to help me with you." I held out the man's card for Zahir's inspection.

"Oh, yes, he is my uncle." Zahir verified everything, and without any trace of fear or trepidation, which I had expected, given Uncle Bouncer's offer to take care of any problems.

I asked incredulously, "So I'm guessing this uncle will come to beat you at my call? Is that his role in your family, to punish people?"

Still smiling, Zahir nodded. "Yes, yes, he does that. And he takes us fishing, also."

Fishing? Beating then fishing?

I left Zahir's private place, shaking my head at this new, unbelievable cultural experience. I climbed up the stairs to share the story with Karen. *What a place to be a principal, with Uncle back-up only a call away.*

In his special confinement with no one to entertain, Zahir completed lots of schoolwork and did well grade-wise. His teachers were impressed.

I decided to release him into the general population after a ten-day stay in his cozy space.

"You understand you can be sent back if you do not manage yourself, right, Zahir?" Karen and I helped him pack up his books.

"Oh, yes, I understand, Mrs. Goolsby. I will control myself. I don't want any more trouble and I miss everyone at ISK."

He almost ran to his classroom, taking the stairs two at a time. Karen and I smiled and crossed our fingers that Zahir's new freedom would last, for all of us.

The staff appreciated his renewed efforts to be a controlled student, and although still recognizable in his goofiness and free flowing comments at times, he definitely turned a corner. The family sent gifts of gratitude for keeping Zahir in the school.

He went on to graduate from ISK years later, and there were many who celebrated his success, his Uncle Bouncer among the applauding crowd.

And no, I never called him for back-up.

Running an American school in Afghanistan called for creativity and openness to new ways of doing things. The methods I knew from my past experiences needed tweaking at times to make sense in this culture.

And I am sure our Afghan and international families felt the same way trying to understand our American way of doing school.

The Unveiled Truth: My go-to strategy for combating problems is to bring wise counselors together, those invested or experienced with the situation, and see what evolves. It takes courage and humility to admit cluelessness, especially as a leader, but I find others are willing to assist when their contributions are wanted and valued.

When we are trying new things, it can take time before we hit upon success, but stubbornly *doing things as they've always been done* also takes time and may produce no positive results.

If your best effort is a failure, dust yourself off and try again. Ask advice of those around you who know you and the situation well, and don't be afraid to try something new. Success may be just around the corner.

What ongoing problem or challenge has yet to change despite your attempts to fix it? What new strategies can you employ? Who are you surveying for possible solutions?

16

The Fine Art of Failure

Living and working with others outside of my comfort zone and familiar turf added challenges beyond basic personality differences and clashes. I found that many of my problems stemmed from *me*, not Afghan traditions or cultures.

The truth of the old saying *it takes one to know one* hit me hard when I realized some of my conflicts and failures were with strong, confident individuals—like me. People who thought they needed to have the final say—like me.

In my daily challenge to champion the standards of ISK while navigating Afghan culture, I made mistakes. Some I made more than once, which is disappointing since I consider myself a seasoned, self-disciplined leader.

One principal-fail happened in my third year with an opinionated, demanding parent. I was standing in the foyer outside my office, in a public space, speaking to Karen. The unfamiliar father entered the building and immediately started speaking to me, bypassing the usual cultural greeting.

"Are you, Mrs. Goolsby, the principal here at ISK? My two children are arriving soon from the U.S. and I must have their enrollment completed today." He barely seemed to take a breath and took no note that I was in conversation with someone else.

"I will be with you in just a minute. Please have a seat." I politely gestured to one of our guest chairs.

He looked that direction but instead of moving to a chair, took a step closer to me.

"I am short on time with other appointments. I require your assistance now." Smiling, like that made it okay, he interrupted me again.

I locked eyes with Karen. Like-minded and assertive herself, she could read what I was feeling. *Rude*. She went to her desk, allowing me the freedom to pick up our conversation another time.

I should have stopped and asked him to step into my office. I should have held my boiling emotions inside. But I didn't. I turned fully to my offender, who was now face-to-face with me as he'd left little space between us in his intimidation game.

"Sir, I do not appreciate your approach here," I began.

The situation escalated quickly when he chose a particular remark that I heard often in parent-pressure interactions: "I don't think you know who you're talking to."

I wanted to scream the same question back, "Do you know who *you* are talking to?"

Instead, I found myself saying, "Well, it looks like you're a father who wants to enroll his students at my school."

Not helpful. Both of us threw words at each other with neither of us listening to the other.

Khalid's office was a floor above mine in the administration building. Soon, I heard him scurrying down the stairs as our verbal debate echoed throughout the marble-floored building. My face, as well as my tone, communicated my anger at this dominating, unreasonable man.

Khalid knew how to defuse these situations, for my good and the good of the school. He wedged himself between me and the father, gently moved him back, and began to speak in Dari, using his expressive eyes and many gestures to bring calm and reassurance to the visitor.

I stopped talking and composed myself. The three of us went into my office and worked out the needs of the family to everyone's satisfaction.

I would love to say I learned my lesson and this type of scene never happened again, but all I can say is it never happened at the same intense level. I learned much from watching Khalid and Byron about not responding defensively.

"Relax. You can't make everyone happy. You don't need to be apologetic about your decisions or ISK procedures either, but if possible, figure out how to help people within our framework." Byron told me this a couple of times in my early years when I sought to convince someone in a verbal exchange that my way was best.

I got better as time went on.

In my seven years of hiring and occasionally firing staff, I had about three landmark failures. One teacher was hired by the Oasis home office before I was placed in the principal role. I doubt I would have offered him the job since his teaching credential had expired. I rarely had to accept a teacher without current licensure and only with the understanding that the employee would correct the situation within two years at the most. This teacher did not make any effort to requalify, one of several issues we butted heads on.

I kept this teacher on for three years, which more than one person in my support system questioned. Looking back, I question the wisdom in that decision, too.

"He is great with the students and in knowing his subject area. But, he doesn't see the need for planning lessons ahead, keeping his grades current, utilizing group work in addition to lecture for student learning, along with the other responsibilities of the teaching profession." My explanation to why he wasn't dismissed in year one or two was always accompanied with a heavy sigh. I hoped things would improve, and sooner rather than later for my sake and that of ISK's students.

We argued over email and in person, matching brain and word power, but not matching desired outcomes. I wanted all required paperwork from lesson plans and accreditation documents, especially grades, posted by deadlines to keep things running smoothly for everyone. I expected on time attendance for all meetings and for him to never leave his classroom unattended, even for a quick copy or cup of coffee.

All teachers needed to employ certain instructional considerations for our varied English-language-learners or distance-learning accommodations for enrolled students when emergencies arose—all of which he refused to do. The list of my concerns and administrative actions recorded against this teacher filled two single-spaced pages by the third year.

Michael and Karen empathized with me about my failure to get this teacher to cooperate but could not make it right for me. They let me vent, and even cry at times when I broke over current frustrations. I leaned heavily on Byron as a veteran administrator and a man, to show me how to deal with this situation. Although he agreed with my assessment of each critical incident and joined me in the heavy-duty discussions with the teacher, he also could not get this young man to respond with respect and cooperation to our expectations, and particularly to respect me as his supervisor.

Consequently, I never felt like a successful principal in light of this teacher's time at ISK. Once he left, I doubt anyone missed our ongoing feud, something I should have managed better, especially on a closed compound. According to his exit summary, he had a terrible experience under my leadership, also. His comments indicated he felt unduly criticized and that my demands were petty, though they were no different than my demands on every other staff member. He claimed he was never sure where he stood with me, and that feeling was mutual. *Sigh.*

Two other teachers who felt I was the worst boss they ever had were drawn to ISK for the cross-cultural experience more than the educational environment. They came later in my tenure and really struggled with the restricted lifestyle.

I felt blocked from forming a quality relationship with these two teachers individually as they entered into a romantic relationship. My offenses seemed to literally double as they took up each other's charges against me. One wanted approval for extra-curricular activities for ISK students that were not feasible or safe, but my explanations only offended. Our policies and security procedures were seen as toxic and unreasonable.

My baby-boomer ethic, which insisted they adhere to our team's mission, fell on deaf millennial ears. My efforts to clear up misunderstandings or work-related requirements were seen as controlling and condescending. I hoped to build bridges in each conversation and memo, but never succeeded with these two and a couple of others from that same entry year. It was a great discouragement to me that I couldn't make a true connection with a few of the younger staff. I found them hard-working and dedicated, in their own way and on their own terms, just not a good fit for ISK with all its unique demands.

I didn't just fail with parents and teachers, but some students needed more than ISK or I could provide.

A politically connected, repatriated Afghan father brought his American-born, teenage son Ahmad to ISK for high school. Usually, students coming to ISK from American schools began whenever they arrived in Afghanistan since we could transfer credits easily. However, Ahmad had attended an international school in Dubai right before coming to Kabul his freshman year, so there were a few additional steps.

During the father's initial visit to my office, I noticed his expensive suit, leather shoes, gold cufflinks, and a diamond-studded wristwatch. He captured my attention with the sad news of his wife's poor health and her absence in this move. She needed more medical attention than Afghanistan offered, so she remained in the U.S.

My compassion for the single dad and lonely son cooled when he threw out some comments which had no bearing on my need-to-know.

"My son is worth millions of dollars as my family's legacy is quite valuable."

Okay, I get it. You are letting me know who I am talking to.

Having a million-dollar student was a first for me, but I took it all in stride and did my job to get a schedule set up for Ahmad. He was a kid, a kid with a sick mom far away and no siblings at home, just a busy working father in Kabul isolation. My heart went out to him before I ever met him in person.

A couple of weeks later, Ahmad came to ISK. He was polite and quiet, which at first seemed a welcome change from the teens who moved to Kabul against their will with obstinate attitudes. But quickly, we saw major issues pop up.

One day, my assistant principal, Ken, came to the admin building from his office in the high school building. "So, Ahmad is racking up the absences. He's taking long weekends in Dubai apparently. And when he is here, he's sleeping in class with his sweatshirt hood pulled over his head. The teachers are asking if he's on drugs or depressed. What do you think?"

Ken handed me an attendance sheet for Ahmad detailing his three to four days per week attendance.

"Wow, this is serious. Have you talked to him?" I handed the sheet back to Ken and watched him take a long drink from his always-present coffee cup while he settled into a chair.

"Yeah, a couple of times. I really like the kid. His social skills are great. You can tell his family has invested in him. But I can't figure out where his apathy is coming from." Ken leaned his tall frame forward and continued with genuine concern. "He told me he goes to visit his older brother in Dubai. Maybe he's just hungry for family. Bet his dad isn't around much. You know how these political guys work and socialize to all hours, letting their house staff take care of the kids at home."

I nodded, having heard this sad story many times during my years of working with the families of MPs and government officials'. But usually these students loved coming to school, being with friends, and having something to do besides sit behind their walled home compounds. Ahmad was not trying to make a life for himself at ISK.

"Well, if anyone can connect with him, it's you, Ken. Continue reaching out to him and keep me posted." Ken drained his coffee cup, gave me a thumbs up, and headed back to his domain.

Ken was incredible with students, particularly young men. He was creative, funny, and *cool* by high schoolers' standards, especially to our Afghan population. Although he was tough, students rarely complained about his expectations or discipline because they recognized he really cared for them.

After calls to the father, strategy sessions with his teachers, and personal chats, Ken was stumped. "Let's talk to him together," he suggested one day after an admin meeting. "Maybe he needs a motherly approach—no offense, Gail."

I saw the twinkle in his eyes, so I let it go. I had made peace with being *the mom of the school* years earlier. "Whatever works. Let's set it up so his classmates don't think he's in trouble, okay?"

Ken and I did our best at this meeting with Ahmad, exchanging our administrators' hats for those of counselor and friend. We offered compassion and understanding for his difficult transition from the U.S. and the loneliness in his Kabul home. Though Ahmad maintained eye contact with us and never responding negatively, he said little.

"I like ISK fine and everyone is great. I have no complaints. Thank you for all your help." Ahmad left my office with Ken, and I hoped our message of care got through and would serve to inspire him to try harder at school.

But nothing changed. His father offered payment for additional tutors at ISK, but Ahmad would not show up for after-school appointments. He was flunking and didn't care.

In an earnest effort to help and as a father of four himself, Ken pressed Ahmad's dad to take more interest in his son. Once, when another student reported that Ahmad was ill and had taken himself to the hospital instead of coming to school, Ken called the dad to check up on the situation.

"That didn't go well," Ken reported to me later that morning when I popped into the high school building with some announcements to distribute. "Ahmad's dad accused me of interfering. I can't win with the kid or the dad." With a sad look that gripped my heart, Ken leaned back in his desk chair and stared out the window. I left his office with a determination to figure out something that would help this situation.

Falling back on my counseling training, I tried to provide for some of Ahmad's emotional needs on a second occasion in my office after the hospital incident. I spoke delicately but openly with him concerning his mother's health back in the U.S. He was tearful and attentive in our conversation, but silent.

Nothing changed in his attendance or classroom performance.

Basically, Ken and I tried to motivate Ahmad in a traditional up-front American style, showing we cared for him personally as well as academically. Sadly, we learned how unacceptable assertive communication can be in an indirect culture like Afghanistan's, even for those who have lived outside the country like Ahmad's family. Once Afghans return to their home country, the traditional behaviors often resurface.

Frustration continued for all involved and with failing grade cards and excessive absences now requiring detention, the father started blaming ISK, specifically Ken and me. The new ISK director, John Brown, who succeeded Byron in 2009, had been brought up-to-date on Ahmad's story and wanted to avoid any Afghan governmental backlash to ISK due to the father's political clout.

One day, Ahmad's father bypassed Ken and me at John's invitation.

As I watched him enter John's office, I got nervous. *Great, how is this going to turn out?*

"I require apologies from everyone for my son's problems. Mr. Jensen and Mrs. Goolsby, and all his teachers. They have spoken to him about family matters that are not their concern. I expected better from such a prestigious school. No one has helped my son as he deserves."

After unloading his list of complaints, he left campus and John delivered the critical message to Ken and me later that day. We were flabbergasted at the accusations after all the time and effort we'd given to this one student. The father was pushing off any personal-parental responsibility for Ahmad's problems fully onto us.

John set up another meeting with senior ISK leadership and the father. Ken and I did our best to humbly express our intentions to assist Ahmad and to apologize, even though it tasted sour in our mouths. The father eventually calmed down and seemed to accept our contrition.

"We have a garden and an inside pool at our home, not far from ISK. I will have you all come for dinner and for swimming. Bring Ahmad's teachers." He stood, shook all our hands with a smile, and left John's office.

"Whew," sighed Ken. "What a relief to have that done. I hope we're headed toward better days with Ahmad."

We all nodded and made our way back to our offices. I was still stinging from the blame-shifting and personal groveling which had taken place, but it'd be worth it if we had helped this troubled teen.

We hadn't.

A few days after that meeting, Ahmad quit coming to

school altogether and our calls were not returned from the father.

What had happened? We thought all was well. Now, we felt like fools and failures. So much invested, so much hoped for.

Classmates of his reported that he had returned to Dubai with his older brother. Hopefully being with his sibling would help him start caring about what he did with the rest of his life.

Did we fail as educators? As caring human beings? As clumsy Americans bumbling through the Afghan culture maze? For many ISK students, shuffled around the world several times in their young lives, the same personal attention bore much fruit and gratitude, but not with Ahmad.

Looking back at all of my principal failures, I would say, if put back in those same situations, I would do many of the same things (minus angry outbursts). Just because the results looked bad, it didn't mean I had been wrong to try, didn't mean I had completely failed. While not producing success for every situation, I always learned lessons for my own growth and improvement.

I learned to do better at holding my tongue, at not voicing my every opinion in every conversation. I learned to listen longer and not start strategizing too quickly. I learned the benefit of humility and initiating reconciliation. I learned there is more than one way to do things right—a very powerful, but hard-to-convince-myself lesson that I have to repeat to myself often. And I learned to study culture, noting the nuances needed to make good connections with others for best results.

I gained from my failures, so none of my efforts were a complete waste.

The Unveiled Truth: Mistakes are not the end of your story. *It's what you do with the mistakes that makes the difference.* I heard this first from my father, then hammered it into my own children and students, too. I attempted to practice what I preached.

If we try to ignore our failures, we'll likely keep stumbling over the same problematic stone embedded in our paths. This wastes precious time. Instead, we should take note and *own* the stone, step onto it, and use it to get a better view of the road leading to our improvement.

Don't let your falls gain you nothing more than a face full of dust.

What recent failure has you paralyzed or too discouraged to continue, and how instead can you use the error for future success?

17

Who's in Charge?

The lessons I learned under Byron equipped me to run a quality school in a difficult place. When he was preparing to leave ISK in June 2009, I was asked about taking the director job again. I gave the same response as when Joe Hale asked me in 2005, "No, thanks."

But where would we find another seasoned educational leader willing to come to Afghanistan?

My husband met John Brown, a congenial American gentleman, through some business connections in Kabul and introduced him to ISK. John was already situated in Afghanistan, had worked with college students in the U.S., and possessed an MBA. He applied for ISK Deputy Director job to train with Byron for the 2009 spring semester and became director the next school year.

Our home office approved his position, but since he had no previous experience with K-12 schools, they advised him to "let

Gail run the school." He was to concentrate on security, budget, and government issues, the same areas of responsibility Byron had carried. I was more than happy to stay focused on textbooks, students, parents, and teachers.

My first inkling of concern came during the overlap of my two bosses, following our required Strategic Planning sessions in December 2008. I'd brought in a close friend and top-quality educational leader to facilitate these important meetings with staff, administration, various school committees, and community stakeholders. Byron determined John should attend the gatherings to learn as much as possible about ISK and tasked him with writing a summary of the three-day outcomes to submit with our accreditation documents.

"Byron wants you to look this over." John entered my office and handed me a single sheet of paper. He took a seat near my desk and looked at me expectantly, though pleasantly.

The large, decorative font in the heading grabbed my attention first. *This looks more like a promotional handout than an official school report.* I pressed through the verbose copy—twice—trying to make sense of the words.

"I'm not sure what you are trying to say here, John." I tried to be diplomatic but clear, feeling protective of this final piece for our accreditation requirements under my leadership. "This doesn't cover most of the important decisions made during this meeting or detail our five-year plan. I'm not sure anyone receiving this will understand all the work we've accomplished this week."

To add to my confusion, John took the paper from my hand with a smile and a slight chuckle, remarking, "Then my work here is finished. Thanks!" He returned to Byron's office while my mouth hung open.

What did John hear me say just now? That I was okay with the report as written? No!

We had accomplished so much in a short time to gain U.S. and Afghan recognition for ISK, and I had hoped Byron would equip his replacement to keep things moving forward. I didn't follow him to Byron's office to voice my concerns, lest I interfere, but I wondered about my new boss's qualifications for the job he was undertaking. And I wondered how that would impact me.

To my relief, John's first year went fairly well with him around the school *all the time*, unlike Byron had been. I thought, "Yes! Finally, I have help." Our personalities were very different, but I thought I would learn more diplomacy and people skills from him as those seemed to be his strengths.

But I also recognized he was not spending time with the people who made the decisions about our USAID funding as Byron had, and again, I wondered how this would work for ISK.

By the time Byron left, I had long fulfilled my initial two-year Oasis commitment. I had stayed two additional years for my MEd degree compensation package. After completing my contractual agreements, I was allowed to determine year by year if I wanted to return. Because of ISK's great impact in Afghanistan, I found myself in an annual paradox.

I don't want to stay, but I can't leave yet.

Finally, Michael and I decided in December 2009 to give two more years to Afghanistan, for his leadership training/English classes and my role at ISK. I would raise up replacements and depart Kabul for good June 2012. By this time, Michael and I had one darling granddaughter, and I wanted to spend more time with my adult children, too.

As time went on with my new boss, I wanted to leave more than I wanted to stay.

Little by little, things began to unravel. Byron had empowered me to handle the day-to-day problem solving, coming to him as needed, but mostly just reporting and keeping him informed. John started making decisions that previously had been my responsibility and meeting with teachers, students, and families by himself. There was widespread confusion over who people should answer to on campus and who made decisions about school issues, unlike the first four years.

The second year with John had many rough spots. When I needed clarification or had questions about his directives, I visited him in private or sent him an email. Sometimes the sheer volume of his words in a face-to-face conversation or in written responses left me more confused than ever.

Once, I was attending an Oasis administrator's conference in West Africa and received an alarming epistle from John detailing how he wanted me to fire Charlene and get another librarian when I returned. In my absence, some issues had him locking horns with our strong-willed book-lady, and in great detail, he informed me she needed to be dismissed.

At first I wanted to shout through the computer, "Are you kidding me? This is so ridiculous." But instead, I wrote one paragraph to his five, basically advising, "You better have good documentation detailing the need for her dismissal. If anyone would know how to take you to task legally over such a decision, it would be Charlene. Otherwise, I suggest you find a way to get along with her. She is a pillar of ISK and I personally don't think there is a comparable replacement. Stubbornness and all, she is an excellent educational professional."

He never brought it up again. But Charlene was not the only staff member who had issues with him.

"I was told by John that I would be mentoring new teachers and helping with grant writing." An experienced American teacher shared this surprising information with me a few months into her first year at ISK. "I've spent most of my weekends investigating possible sources for grants, but nothing is being followed up on by John. I thought I would be part of the school leadership team like I was back home, so I feel like I was basically lied to. I enjoy teaching, but I am wasting some of my skills that could be helping the school more. I'm pretty frustrated." Her face was tight, unsmiling.

My wide-eyed expression confirmed what she had already figured out.

"You didn't know about any of these arrangements he made with me, did you?"

"Absolutely not!" I felt my face get hot. I had hired her to teach various classes like girls' PE/Health, oral communication, and a couple of top-level science classes, which she did with excellence. "I don't know what to tell you, except I'm sorry you are disappointed. I wouldn't have wanted that to happen."

"It isn't your fault. You gave me the exact classes you mentioned when you hired me. I figured out the disconnect pretty quickly. But, yes, I am disappointed in these empty promises he made to me. Don't worry, I will fulfill my contract to the end of the year. There is plenty of significant work to be done here." She patted my hand and we remained on good terms, even after she left ISK.

I felt anger and distrust for John well up more frequently as time went on. I fought the negative emotions toward my boss through prayer and counsel with my husband. The two of us determined we needed to establish a better relationship with John and arranged for a long visit one evening to hear his personal story. He didn't seem interested in listening to our story, but we did gain insight into his background and personal life challenges, which helped—a bit.

I began to feel paranoid and insecure about my position. Now officed upstairs, I could see teachers and students coming and going from John's office but had no idea what was being discussed. John avoided conversation with me unless absolutely necessary.

"I told him he needed to stop going around you, but he's intimidated, I guess," Ken said with a wry grin. "You are tough, you know."

I had stepped into Ken's office for advice on finding a way forward in the relational mire I'd gotten into with John. Our tense relationship was impacting everyone in our small ISK universe.

"I am working through this myself, although John seems more open to me as a guy, apparently. I have heard from other female teachers on campus that they feel he talks down to them at times and their opinions are dismissed." Ken leaned back in his chair and rubbed his hands over his bald head with a serious look now erasing the earlier grin.

"I don't know what I can do differently besides try to talk things out." I shifted uncomfortably in my chair. "He seems agreeable in our conversations, though I'm left uncertain what he's expecting of me sometimes. And it's hard to communicate an unclear plan to the team."

Shaking my head in discouragement, I left Ken's office with the small comfort that I was not the only person confused and frustrated.

I felt the unsteady school pulse keenly. I observed the students, the staff, the finances, the relationships with USAID, and the standards of excellence so painstakingly established begin to falter. In early 2011, I drew up my succession plan and training schedule so that everything would be in place before my departure, now one year away.

The seven-week summer break before my last year included Anna's wedding in late June 2011. It was a wonderful family celebration and a fun time of relaxing back in the States. But in July, my restful vacation turned stressful after a series of emails and phone calls from John redefined my role at ISK from principal to *Senior Academic Advisor*. I could not make sense of everything he said, but clearly he wanted major changes. I offered to resign, but he said that wasn't what he wanted.

But what is an Academic Advisor exactly? Who ever heard of such a position at a K-12 school?

I felt like I was being sidelined. I sat in my Missouri home often in tears and unable to sleep, my mind racing through troublesome potential scenarios. Michael did his best to help me see my way through this quagmire, and we spent many hours praying together and trying to strategize how I might have a successful final year. I became so worried about how things would go in Kabul that many of my family and friends urged me not to return.

"You've done enough. Six years in Afghanistan is significant. Let it go," one of my sending team supporters tried to offer as a solution to my crisis.

No, I could do this. After six years, what was one more? It would be all right. How bad could it get?

After the rough phone and email exchanges, I knew I faced trouble ahead at my return in early August. I decided to press on with mentoring Celeste, who had been at ISK from the early years as a teacher and Literacy Coach, now moving into the role of Elementary Principal. I also needed to train another school counselor in the fall, my third since ISK started. Though Ken would remain in the States until February on family leave, we planned for him to take complete responsibility of the high school by spring of 2012.

The fall term brought even more stress than I'd anticipated as we adopted a new web-based school information management system. The new IT Director had some experience with the system but not in electricity-weak, internet-starved Afghanistan. Problem after problem kept teachers and administrative assistants frustrated. Karen had left ISK in June 2011, so her expertise was not available and sorely missed, especially by me. Negative attitudes popped up around campus and computer/internet issues wore everyone down.

Finances at ISK began a downward spiral after the first five years. USAID kept us routinely nervous with slow disbursements of award money, demands for audits, and threats of ending all funding in the changing U.S. political climate. Trying to keep tuition costs fair for all families was a nightmare. It seemed impossible to establish a sustainable budget with all the variables thrown at us, such as security threats, unreasonable landlords, fewer international families, high turnover of students, and increased costs for everything as the country modernized.

"Please, Mrs. Goolsby, can you take my tuition money?" I looked at the fifth grader holding out a handful of Ben Franklins as I supervised the morning car-line. "We haven't received our contract, and my father is afraid I will be dismissed from ISK if we don't pay now."

This type of incident began happening in early September and by the end of October, two-thirds of ISK families were still in the dark about their tuition costs. I was feeling constant pressure to explain the unexplainable, and staff clamored for more IT assistance to do their jobs. To ease the chaos, I felt pushed to find solutions with my boss. Unfortunately, the more I asserted my concerns and opinions about the state of the campus, the more trouble I created. For me.

"Finances and IT are not your responsibility," John responded to my questions, strongly.

"From my perspective, everything pertaining to ISK is my business. I cannot do my job with these huge issues unsolved," I responded, also strongly. This was a couple of weeks into October and the tension between the two of us was becoming clear to many.

Under the guise of needing close proximity to the novice school counselor in the high school building down the street, and with Ken not there as an administrative presence, I turned over my admin building office to Celeste. I hoped with some physical distance, things might cool off between John and me.

I enjoyed more time to hang out with the older students, many I had known all my years at ISK. Teens in Afghanistan are not as standoffish with their teachers and principals as Western students tend to be. In the morning gathering time outside, students would strike up easy conversations with me. Here I knew my role and felt confident. Even relaxed.

"So, Yusef, I am concerned for your health. Are you well?" I walked over to a small group of senior students. The group turned to greet me and shake hands in respect.

"Why, yes, of course, I am well, Mrs. Goolsby. Why do you ask?" Yusef looked quizzically at me.

"Well, I can see that your pants no longer fit, they are so large. Surely you have lost much weight, so I wondered if you'd been sick lately." I kept my expression sincere, but soon Yusef and his companions grasped my meaning. His sagging trousers, American style, were against the dress code for ISK.

The young men laughed and poked their guilty classmate as his face blushed. "I am sorry, Mrs. Goolsby. I will not wear them again, I promise."

"Thank you, Yusef, for saying so, but since this is not the first time you have made this mistake, I need you to go into the office and call for your mother to send a different pair of pants so you can remain in school today. Please go now. Gentlemen, have a good day." Amidst jostling their friend, they returned farewell waves to me with smiles and nods of respect.

This was my world still, and some things remained clear to me. I needed to stay focused on students and teachers, caring and investing for their growth and development.

In early November 2011, I had several serious encounters with John. Some he initiated, and some I did. After one particularly adversarial session, I knew we were in crisis mode.

"Come to my office in thirty minutes," John's voice stated over my cell phone early on a weekend night as I lounged on the couch watching a video.

I told Michael where I was headed. Neither of us took this to be a casual meeting but had no idea what the agenda would be. I was nervous as I walked across the street from my apartment to the admin building.

Unbeknownst to me, Michael followed me, staying downstairs in the foyer. The conversation escalated fairly quickly.

"What do you mean you think I should leave? Are you firing me? You have never given me a list of deficiencies to even know what to improve upon." I felt my temper rising as John suggested he'd rather I go home immediately than wait for my contract to run out in June.

"This is not about your skills as a principal or lack of attention to work responsibility. This has to do with our inability to work together," he responded with equal intensity, something

I had not seen often. "I need someone who follows my directives word-for-word and without question."

"So, let me get this straight. I hire a campus full of professionals to teach critical thinking to our students, but I should not exercise that in a leadership role?" I shot back, among other remarks, likely not well filtered or respectfully communicated in my highly agitated state.

After a few more rounds of back and forth, I shook my head at our conversation going nowhere. "Why don't we get some mediation from the home office or someone in our international community? Pick anyone with whom you'd feel comfortable. There has to be a way to deal sanely with our issues so the stability of ISK is not threatened."

A steely expression accompanied his negative response.

I stumbled back home in a dazed, wobbly state and retreated straight upstairs to my bedroom to avoid seeing Charlene, who was now our housemate in the latest campus housing shift. Michael followed me in from the living room and closed the door.

I crumpled into a chair and started to cry, my face in my hands to muffle the sound.

He knelt beside me. "I know, hon. I know what happened. I heard everything from the downstairs foyer. You are not going to meet with him alone again." He held me and let me cry for a long time. The next days were painful and stressed, and I kept to myself as much as possible, still doing my job as best I could.

The morning of our departure with Charlene for our China trip, several days after that weekend encounter, John called me back to his office and allowed Michael to attend. He repeated his plan to dismiss me. We requested mediation again, with Michael suggesting the international church pastor as an unbiased, godly facilitator.

John refused. He was done. He had already drafted my separation conditions, including a small severance package to help me financially.

I had no viable recourse. I signed the papers and we rose to leave in a fog of disbelief.

"When you return from fall break, you need to decide if you will leave immediately or at Christmas. June is not an option." We heard these parting words from John as we left his office.

Michael held tightly to my hand as we silently retrieved our suitcases and joined Charlene at the waiting ISK vehicle to take us to the Kabul airport. No one spoke as we gazed out the windows at familiar sights along the dusty roads. I dared not make eye contact in the rearview mirror with our driver, a caring national worker who likely knew trouble was brewing but would not ask any questions in proper respect for our positions at ISK. I worried the concern in his eyes would start my tears flowing again and that would be too much for any of us to endure in the moment.

Escape was just what I needed, Michael and Charlene, too. This vacation would give me seven days to ponder my plight and plan my next step.

The Unveiled Truth: I heard as a young adult that there are two aspects to every job. There's the job itself with the responsibilities and skills required. But there is also *who you work for.*

Before ISK, I had already encountered this truth with

several great and not-so-great bosses and leaders. But the clash with John was unlike any other regarding how much it affected those around me and my own emotional state. I was challenged to a whole new level to figure out how to deal with seemingly impossible relationships and situations.

When relational problems peak, we can only do what we can do. Reconciliation takes two willing parties to happen. Forgiveness is something we can do alone—and we must, to preserve our connection to God and prepare our hearts to genuinely care for our offender.

If relational failure hits your life, do your best to act well and not add to your list of errors. Later you can figure out what part you played and what was outside your control. With the intention to learn from the mistakes, the pain can be turned to your gain.

Who are you struggling to maintain a positive relationship with today, and what actions can you take to display integrity in the midst of the trial?

18

Making the Best of a Bad Situation

When I returned from China, I told John I wanted to stay till the end of the semester to mentor my replacements.

He told me I could not continue with my principal duties or train my successors until we established all the details of my departure and maybe not at all. I lived directly across from the admin building, and the classroom buildings neighbored my apartment. I could eat my meals as usual in the staff dining room and use exercise equipment in the Marble Mansion, but basically, during the day, I was under house arrest.

With such a close community on the ISK campus, I knew an announcement needed to happen immediately to squash speculations. My educator friend from back home, who knew the campus situation well, offered to assist me in writing a statement to read to the staff.

I emailed her three single-spaced pages full of defensive

explanations. She recognized my need to vent and then wisely led me to whittle down my emotional words to three brief paragraphs that I read on November 15th to the full ISK staff:

> As all of you know, this year was planned to be my last one at ISK. A change has occurred in that now I will be leaving Dec 19th, at John's request. I want to assure you that this is not due to moral failure on my part, but beyond that I will not be answering any questions. I ask you to please respect my privacy on this.
>
> For the remaining four weeks, I will be focusing on mentoring the school counselor and assisting the secondary teachers and students in their day-to-day needs. Beginning January, I will continue to be available via email as needed.
>
> Let me close in saying, these past years have been incredible working with dedicated professionals like you. It has been the opportunity of a lifetime and I am honored to have served with you. Elementary team, you have a major blessing in Celeste and she knows much more about being a principal than I ever have! I love what you do with the little ones and appreciate how you are training them up so well. Secondary team, the Jensen Magic is coming back in February...you are in for a treat at his return. Together you will take the teenagers at ISK to higher levels of achievement and character formation, I know it.
>
> Thank you for allowing me to be part of your lives and this amazing ISK adventure.

I held my emotions together through the reading and then exited immediately to my apartment. I felt a major stress attack coming on and was glad for the short distance home. Once safely in my bedroom, I sat in the late afternoon shadows in complete silence and solitude. I didn't answer Charlene's or Michael's soft knocks on my door.

What transpired with the staff following my announcement is unknown to me except through bits of gossip. Many assertive team members spoke strongly and would not gloss over the impact of this decision. I wondered if John thought the team would be pleased with his choice to remove me. Judging by the mass exodus of staff months later, I would guess they did not agree. He won, but he also lost.

"Hey, how are you doing today?" Celeste braved daily visits to check on me. "Got a few questions for you, if that's okay?" She sat at the kitchen table with me and took the mug of hot tea I had ready for her.

There was no doubt in my mind she was at risk by visiting me so often. During the weeks leading up to my departure, I grew in my appreciation of her as a mature, dependable educator as she sought to help teachers keep teaching while they dealt with student/parent questions about my absence. She did not share inappropriately during our chats, just offered her presence and understanding and asked for my input on various school procedures and issues.

More than once we cried and prayed together, for me, for her, and for ISK which we both loved so much.

The international pastor in Kabul asked Michael and me to meet with him. He wanted to help with the apparent ISK crisis as it had impacted his congregation. The Christian community was a tight group of about 300 expats, united in their desire to help Afghans and each other. Under the Afghan Constitution, foreigners possessed religious freedom as long as they did not attempt to convert Afghans away from Islam.

We walked the few blocks to the church grounds in the

second week of my confinement. It felt great to leave campus. In the safe environment of his office, I poured out the details.

"Wow. That is incredible. And John is not willing to have any of the international community assist toward reconciliation? What about your home office?" our friend asked.

"No, he is done," I replied, looking down at my hands in shame. "He feels I was not loyal to him and my direct personality was too combative. The Oasis leaders are backing him, letting him make the decision in regard to me. They have not given me any audience to share my side of things which really hurts after working for them for almost seven years." I let my gaze drift out through the room's large window to the Kabul mountains in the distance.

He asked a few more questions, mostly about my state of being. I will always remember his next words.

"Gail, you need to leave now. Don't wait for December 19th. This is not a safe place for you given the broken trust between you two. You cannot heal here. And the rest of the team cannot begin their recovery until you are gone. Every time they see you, it makes them review the pain of a situation they cannot fix." He spoke slowly but deliberately, looking at me and then at Michael to check our responses.

As he spoke, the screen door near the picture window swung open just slightly. The idea of leaving Kabul took on the form of this gentle breeze floating in, bringing fresh air, and inviting me to walk through the open door. I nodded my head, with slow tears spilling out.

Michael walked close to me back to the ISK campus, not holding my hand as culture forbade, but trying to show his comfort and support. "I agree, dear, you should go home as soon as possible. Let's check flights tonight and see what we can find."

"Changing an international flight might be expensive, and I don't want Celeste and the new counselor to feel abandoned. They might need help at the semester's close." Even as I made these comments, I felt I would leave as our friend suggested. My heart lifted for the first time in weeks.

A few hours later, I made all the new travel arrangements easily and spent only fifty dollars in extra fees. My new departure date was December 5th, arriving home before Anna's and my birthdays on the 7th and 8th. Only two weeks remained to endure my painful reality until I departed Kabul, for good.

I felt strongly the need to say goodbye to the students before leaving ISK. At first, John denied my request, but then he granted access at two gatherings of students near the end of November. Nothing was said to me about the assemblies in detail, so I just assumed John would tell the students what was happening from his perspective, and I would at least see them one last time.

Celeste came to my apartment to accompany me that afternoon which helped ease my nerves, now in high stress mode. She greeted me with a hug and a Diet Coke, arriving about fifteen minutes before the first assembly. We sat at the kitchen table and sipped our sodas.

"So, did you figure out what you're going to say?" she asked casually.

"What do you mean?" I looked at her incredulously and put my can down hard enough cola came out of the top and spilled onto the table. "I'm supposed to *speak*? No one told me that!" I searched her face while heat flooded my own features. My heartbeat ramped up even more.

Celeste's expression revealed her anger at the lack of John's communication. She looked directly at me and spoke calmly, "Okay. Take a few minutes and think about it. You can do this.

The students love you and will receive whatever you want to say from your heart. Forget about John. Think about them."

I nodded and squelched my rising screams of frustration with thoughts of those dear, innocent faces about to come into view for the last time. I put on my headscarf and checked my make-up in the hall mirror. We walked the very short distance to the assembly area.

The familiar lines of students and teachers crowding onto their chairs and designated spots on the floor reminded me of all the times I had stood in this place over the years to open ISK's weekly programs on character traits. What I modeled now would speak louder than any of my previous scripted lessons on being a productive citizen or faithful friend.

The teachers stood against the back walls as usual to keep their young charges in view and maintain order. Only this time, they did not look in my direction, but kept their faces down with unreadable expressions. I suddenly felt so alone, and awkward. *What do they think of me and my situation?* Paranoia tried to creep into my already overwrought mind. I pushed it aside to face the task at hand.

Celeste and I moved to the front of the assembly room where John was already present, chatting and joking with students as they entered like all was a normal day. We did not make eye contact. Celeste got the students orderly and turned the microphone over to John.

John sat on a stool and read a prepared statement, not adjusting the language for the young students who clearly did not understand his message. When he finished, I stepped in front of the silent, staring crowd of curious, concerned faces. I stood close enough not to need the microphone.

Taking a deep breath I did what I loved to do with students, I told a story.

"Once there was a woman who moved far away from her home. She left her family and country to come to work at a school in Afghanistan to help students learn—not just reading, writing, and math—but how to live well."

My audience nodded and began to smile when they recognized the woman in the story was me. I interjected anecdotes of fun school events and memories, and their eyes sparkled in recollection of the good times we had shared.

"Now, the woman's plan has changed. Instead of leaving at the end of the school year, she is leaving next week." My voice shook a bit at these words. Smiles turned to frowns and little gasps moved through the young crowd.

"No, no, Mrs. Goolsby, don't leave!" One little boy spoke up with large brown eyes filling with tears. Other students began to cry, and teachers moved to keep them calm.

As a counselor, parent, and educator, I recognized the key to helping children through this difficult time was to model composure and confidence both in word and facial expression.

"Now, now, ISK students, hear me. Everything will be okay. You will be okay. Your teachers are still here to help you every day." Small heads nodded weakly in compliance to my leading.

Once I was finished speaking, I stood by the door to receive hugs and squeeze little hands as the classes filed out. I kept a smile fixed firmly, though my emotions were close to erupting. Such precious children, so dear. Some of the teachers touched my arm or gave me a weak smile of encouragement as they left.

Returning to stand by Celeste, she put her arm around me briefly to offer strength. John stayed on his stool and nothing was said while we waited for the next gathering.

Assembly group number two entered, grades seven

through twelve, a much tougher crowd to fool. By now, rumors and questions about my absence had been circulating. I felt pierced by all the dark eyes riveted on me.

I maintained a pleasant expression while John read from his paper once again. Unlike the little ones, the students grasped the meaning. I was leaving ISK. Girls covered their faces with their headscarves to hide their tears. Boys clenched fists and shook their heads. Murmuring began and teachers moved to hush the crowd as I took my place to speak.

"You all know how we constantly talk with you about your future—about the importance of making plans and goals to benefit the most from your efforts? Well, I want to share with you some of my plans and also about how plans can change."

I told the story of visiting Afghanistan in 2004 with Michael and meeting the KIA teachers. I summarized the journey to move to Kabul and become the principal of ISK. I again interjected fun stories of the early years and used student names for connection with the group. We smiled and even laughed over some of the memories.

"My plan was to preside over the graduation of the 2012 Class; however, that has changed. But, hear this! Though my plan is different, yours remains the same. Be the best student you can be, no matter who the principal is. Graduate from ISK and go to college. Use the foundation you gained here in academics and character development to build a bright future. Do it for yourself, your family, your country, your school—for me. Make me proud. I will be looking for news of your accomplishments. I will not forget this time we have spent together. Thank you for the honor of being your principal."

This time, I left the assembly area before the students. I knew I could not hold my feelings in any longer. I retreated to my apartment sanctuary once more. The next forty-five minutes, I released the built-up emotions from the afternoon in my closed bedroom, pacing and sobbing, and at times yelling.

"This is so unfair, God! What did I do to deserve this horrible treatment? All these years living and working in such a hard place and this is how it ends? Aaargh!"

I was wildly angry. I can hardly recall such a deep agony, not even when my mother died unexpectedly a decade earlier. When the fervor subsided, I blew my nose, curled up on my bed, and pulled the covers over my head. I wanted to disappear.

I did not go to dinner that night at the campus dining hall. Michael and Charlene checked on me but gave me the solitude I craved. Celeste filled them in on the afternoon's events.

Surprisingly, I got one more chance to say goodbye to the students and parents a couple of days later. Without asking John's permission, the music teacher plotted to have me sit on stage and narrate the fall elementary music program.

Celeste knew the plan and organized a school-wide reception for me since parents would be on campus. After the concert, Celeste spoke kind words to the audience about my investment in ISK over the past years. Delicious food and attractive decorations were arranged in a large classroom. I received lovely gifts, flowers, cards, hugs, and verbal expressions of appreciation, some through student translators on behalf of their parents. That was another exhausting yet important piece of my leaving well.

The staff wanted an evening together before I left. One of the off-campus teachers offered her home. Everyone I hoped would be there came, and those I hoped would not be in attendance, were not. What a relief. I wasn't sure how that was accomplished, but I was grateful. There were expatriate community friends present, also.

The group presented me with a collection of pictures and personal notes in a bound album along with a large, hardback book of professional photographs of Afghanistan from decades past to the present. Michael thankfully made sure to get a photo of me with each staff member and friend, which I hadn't the energy to orchestrate.

One of my ISK treasures, now matted, framed, and hanging in my dining room, was created by one of the art teachers. She drew a tree trunk and supporting branches in charcoal on a large parchment page, and then obtained a stamped fingerprint "leaf" from all 300 plus students at ISK. She wrote a poem entitled *The Giving Tree,* to accompany the artwork and describe my contribution to ISK.

A surprising final goodbye, after several home visits to close friends off campus, happened on the Presidential Palace grounds a couple of days before my departure.

The Mayor of Kabul, the Minister of Education, and two ISK dads involved with national security hosted the luncheon in a private dining room on the palace grounds. The four gentlemen focused their attention on Michael and me, talking with appreciation about our years of work in the country, and asking about our family and plans after leaving Kabul. They presented us with impressive leather gifts, a handbag for me and an attaché satchel for Michael, each bearing an embossed seal of Afghanistan. I overcame my embarrassment at being the center of attention when I realized the other teachers in attendance had known of this ahead of time and delighted in my being recognized for my work in Afghanistan.

As we departed the party, one of the host dads asked about my flight plans. When he discovered Michael would be leaving a couple of weeks after me, he said, "I would like to send a car to take you to the airport. It would be my pleasure."

I started to politely decline the offer, but Michael spoke up. "That would be very kind. Thank you." He looked at me with a wink, and I nodded acceptance to our host.

The luxurious SUV and driver arrived mid-day on December 5th. He loaded my overweight luggage and invited Michael to accompany me on the drive and be returned to our apartment later. I slipped away from campus earlier than I had announced. With school in full operation, only a few students and staff waved me a final farewell. That was fine with me. My emotions were spent. I was ready to go home.

We moved through the city traffic without stopping at any intersection and maneuvering freely through crowded streets. Michael whispered that the car had special license plates that gave us clearance as a government vehicle. *Very cool!*

Forget parking out in the far lot and making the tiresome journey through checkpoints and security pat-downs that I had endured for years at Kabul's airport. The driver pulled up to the far end of the airport where I had never been before, unloaded my luggage, and then led us to the VIP lounge. He alerted some well-dressed attendants of our presence. He would wait at the vehicle until Michael was ready to return to campus.

We sat on the comfortable, un-Afghan leather couch and immediately received some hot chai in glass cups. Flat screen TVs around the room displayed CNN and one other local language news channel for the sparse occupants. Attendants politely gathered my passport, ticket information, and luggage to check me in as I remained relaxed on the couch.

I giggled to Michael at the pampering. "Thank you for not

letting me refuse this treat. I had no idea this airport oasis existed."

We sat holding hands, discreetly, and saying very little. Then Michael leaned close and whispered, "I'm glad to be sending you home. I know your friends and John and Anna are eagerly waiting to hug you and take care of you. I will finish up my leadership coaching and English classes and be home before Christmas, so it won't be long."

I could only nod and grip his hand tighter. *I am going home —for good.* What a sweet, ultimate comfort to my oh-so-weary soul.

After several minutes, the attendant returned with my stamped passport, luggage claim tags, and boarding pass. He reported my total baggage weight, well over the allowed limit, but without any extra fees required. Another sweet parting gift.

Michael left with the driver when I was escorted to a small security check trailer and then to a van that took me straight to the plane. I walked up the steps, took my seat, and gazed out the window for my last look at Afghanistan.

I was not sad to leave. I was relieved.

The Unveiled Truth: I don't believe in quitting or running away from tough situations, but I am also a realist.

We all need to willingly take ownership of the part we play in a problem and try to reconcile peacefully, but when there is more than one person involved, complete control of any situation is out of the question. Seeking counsel and allowing others to help isn't always easy, but it's wise. Our strained emotions can block a clear view of the conflict, so outsiders are often more rational.

When there is nothing you can do to make a situation better, finish your duties as well as you can, exit with dignity, and let it go. Life is too short to waste on the impossible, and each day offers a fresh page, with no mistakes present, to start again.

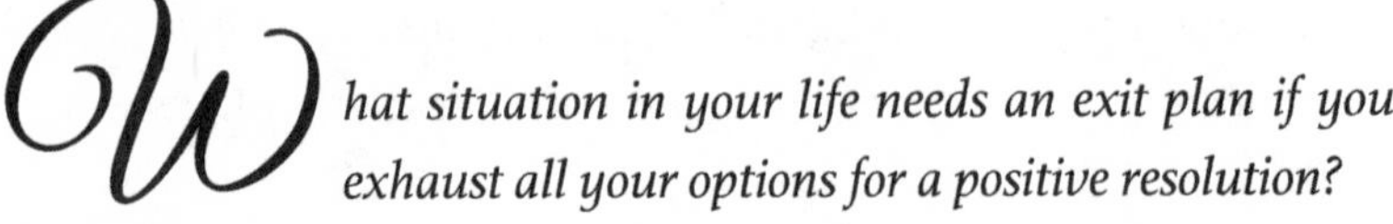

What situation in your life needs an exit plan if you exhaust all your options for a positive resolution?

19

There's No Place like Home to Heal

A small crowd of friends gathered near my children John, Anna, and Jordan (Anna's husband) at the Kansas City airport when I landed December 6, 2011. It was late at night and I was exhausted from two days of travel, so there were quick hugs and words of encouragement from my friends before they left to drive back to St. Joseph, an hour away.

I cannot describe the joy I felt at being done with living two lives. My time in headscarves and tunics was over. The battle with John was in the past. The four of us stood close together waiting for my baggage, and Anna wiped away tears of happiness.

Anna and I love to celebrate our December birthdays together and that year we chose to travel to Branson, Missouri where our family often vacationed. The entire town of Branson, along with Silver Dollar City, an old-timey amusement park, is covered with lights and Christmas decorations. The slow pace and holiday spirit worked its magic to make me feel lighter, to help me forget my troubles.

Back home, I decorated the house and Christmas tree, two of my favorite creative outlets. With festive music blaring from morning to night, I hummed along and felt peace slowly returning.

During the first week of my homecoming, a small cylinder package appeared in the mailbox with no personal return address. It contained a vinyl wall decal that rolled out to read: *There's No Place Like Home.* That touched my wounded heart and made me smile. I wondered who sent it.

I soon solved the mystery when one of my hometown supporters emailed me to ask how I was doing.

I wrote back. "Did you send me a gift in the mail?"

"Yes! I thought of you when I saw it. Seemed to fit your situation perfectly," she responded.

She was so right. I found the perfect place to mount the banner in our study where many family photos were displayed. I enjoyed my first cup of tea each morning in a cozy bathrobe in my favorite armchair gazing at the sweet sentiment.

Christmas and family are great distractors, but as a trained counselor, I knew I needed to pursue debriefing exercises and therapy for my complete recovery. Experts say it takes years to fully decompress from hyper-vigilant situations like we'd endured. The adversarial atmosphere with my boss had only added additional pain.

I needed serious restoration.

In January, I visited my daughter Sarah and her family in Kentucky to help with childcare while her husband taught an intensive, month-long class at Asbury Theological Seminary.

Sarah offered to schedule a time for me to see a counselor. I said, "Yes, sign me up! Let's plan on six sessions."

I walked the short distance to the counselor's office each week in small-town Wilmore, sometimes twice. She was a gentle person. I hardly remember much of what she said, only the wonderful sensation of releasing my recent hurts and disappointments.

She suggested various journal assignments between sessions. One was to unload as many feelings as I could identify, positive and negative, about my departure from Kabul and my last weeks at ISK. The journaling was insightful and didn't stretch me beyond what I could bear. However, another of her assignments pushed me further than I wanted to go.

"You want me to do what? List every single offense I endured during my three years with John? That is seriously the most depressing thing I can think of to do! Really?" I was being rather dramatic, but I didn't want to tackle the task.

"C'mon, you're a counselor," she gently prodded. "You know if you're to gain any relief in your work to forgive John, you need to uncover everything you're forgiving him for. You can do this." She smiled encouragingly while I gathered my stuff to leave. "See you next week."

I filled three journal pages with issues I had with John, writing as fast as the memories came to me as I sat alone in my guest room at Sarah's house. I felt acid pool in my gut as I wrote out what I perceived to be John's accumulated leadership failures.

Then it hit me.

He didn't have much chance to succeed with me. I judged him early on and gathered supporting evidence in my own mind to convict him of poor performance. Was he really as bad as I'd concluded? Good grief.

During our third session, the counselor remarked, "Hearing more about your experience, I figured out who you remind me of."

"Really? Who?" I balanced my tea mug and settled into her comfortable loveseat.

"A war veteran. The unique combination of the high-level stress and thrill of the experience is common to both of you. Your time there was something you wouldn't want to repeat but will never be able to duplicate in normal life. Very interesting."

I nodded my head in agreement with her assessment.

There will never be another Kabul time for me, and at this moment, that comforts me. Though in the future, might I feel differently?

During our month of meetings, I wrote in my journal, read recommended books on forgiveness, and tried to keep focused on growing from the Kabul experience. In the pleasant winter weather, I pushed my granddaughter's stroller on daily walks and let the fresh air, exercise, and sunshine work on my physical restoration to balance my emotional expenditures.

I knew what happened was not all John's fault, however easy laying all the blame on him would have been. I determined to figure out how to keep this type of conflict from occurring in my life again.

"I know what you're wanting," the counselor said to me one day. "You're looking for a list of actions or skills to master so you can avoid any future clashes. But surely you know as a counselor yourself that it isn't that simple. It is an inside-out job. Our attitudes must change, our expectations must change, and our heart must change toward others, and then our behaviors change."

I sighed and nodded, while fresh tears fell. I knew she was

right, but I was anxious to believe I could overcome this trauma as easily as the healing of a broken arm, hoping I'd end up better and stronger than before.

The Oasis leadership invited Michael and me to debrief at the home office at the end of January. President Joe Hale had sent a few emails during and after the peak of conflict with John. In the letter accompanying the invitation to the debriefing, he reiterated the organization's policy to back their directors, yet expressing regret at the difficult situation I had experienced.

However, he also remarked that I was definitely part of the problem and reminded me of my complaints and struggles with Byron, too. With his painful judgment of my character in mind, but hoping to find peace with my brokenness and failure, we went to Southaven and met for three hours with senior leaders of Oasis.

"We're very sorry, Gail, but we are just not resourced to fly home office personnel to our nineteen schools whenever problems like this arise. We'd hoped you and John would work it out and gave him our full support to determine the best course for ISK." Joe began with these words as the five of us sat in a circle of chairs in his comfy office, decorated with items from countries around the world where Oasis schools existed.

"With financial stewardship in mind, we declined to send someone as you requested to choose which of you would leave and who would stay." Joe completed his remarks and looked expectantly at Michael and me for understanding.

Our response changed his expression to shock and surprise.

"That's what John told you? That I wanted you guys to pick who to fire?" I almost spat the words from my mouth.

"Yes," replied Joe slowly. "Is that not correct?" He leaned forward and the other two men looked directly at us.

"I was present during that conversation with John, and what Gail asked for was *mediation*." Michael spoke evenly, but firmly, able to avoid the paralyzing flood of emotions I was dealing with on my side of the couch. "She asked for someone, either you all via Skype or someone in the Kabul community that John would be comfortable with, to help them work things out. She made no demand for you guys to fly out or choose between them."

Silence followed in the room as the new information sunk in.

"Well, we realize the school has gone through difficult times recently." Joe sat back and seemed to want a different direction in the conversation. "I plan to go over in the spring with Khalid, so I can help the staff end a tough year well." His expression looked pleased as he outlined his mission of care.

Michael looked earnestly at Joe and then spoke profoundly. "With all due respect, Joe, if you have the resources to travel to Kabul in the spring with Khalid, which sounds like a pleasant plan, why would you not have spent that same money to help alleviate the trouble that caused the staff their angst in the first place? Maybe the spring compassion tour would not be necessary if the fall crisis had been averted."

I glanced at my husband with awe and appreciation. *Great question! I wish I had thought of that!* I looked over at Joe who seemed to be having the same *aha* moment of reason.

"I guess that's a good question, Michael. When you put it that way, I understand I may have been short-sighted in all this. We lacked some important information on our side of things and didn't ask enough questions." Joe was conciliatory, if not completely apologetic.

The other men made comments and asked questions. I went on to say all that I wished I could have said back in the fall about my concerns for ISK and the instability in the current leadership operations.

"I am not saying I acted well in all aspects under John. I recognize that we had many differences in personality and school leadership expectations. I really wanted to work it out so I could stay until June, but I needed help. I had no local school board or advisors to bring into the situation, and I couldn't stay quiet with so many things crumbling around me at ISK. In my panic, I'm sure I acted even worse. I am sorry for my part in this fiasco." I dabbed my runny nose and tried to make eye contact with the three men as much as possible. But guilt and embarrassment at my failure pulled my gaze to my lap for most of my confession.

One of the leaders who had more direct supervision of Oasis school leaders than Joe spoke privately to me and Michael before we left headquarters.

"I want you to hear this, Gail, that we do appreciate and respect the hard work you did for ISK and Oasis in Afghanistan. You deserved a better ending for those years of sacrifice. Please take my words of sincere apology on behalf of the organization for your sense of not being supported. That was an error on our part." He looked directly at me while offering these words, and with tears, I nodded my acceptance.

The drive back to Missouri was long, and we both felt spent from the emotional output. Yet the chance to say what had been boiling up and over for so many months was a cleansing piece of my healing. I was heard and could let others take from my words whatever they wanted.

Oasis sent both of us to a weeklong conference in March dedicated to helping overseas workers make a healthy transition back to the U.S. We flew to Colorado Springs and participated with a dozen other people returning from various global locations. Each morning, we met with our trained facilitators, working through the common challenges of cultural re-adaptation, forming new identities, and reconnecting with families and friends. The afternoons were open to personal reflection through assignments suggested by our leaders, walks along the scenic mountain paths behind our retreat center, and needed rest.

I journaled as openly and honestly as I could about my pain, my shortcomings, my needs to move forward, and how to access God's wisdom in all these reflections. Believing He made me and established a destiny for my life made Him the perfect counselor and healer for all my personality/behavioral issues. The TV-less, quiet mountain environment helped me hear His voice of correction, but also receive comfort and inspiration for my future.

During one writing exercise in Colorado, I listed all the ways God had proven His care for me between the months of August and December 2011. I love to review the two dozen items even today. They include things like living with Charlene, the November China trip, Celeste's friendship, gifts from ISK families and staff, the VIP treatment at the airport, and Karen's and Ken's visits to my home before Christmas when I returned. All were precious gifts to a wounded heart.

That week in Colorado was a needed piece for our renewal. More for me than Michael who wasn't sure if he was staying stateside or going back to Kabul.

When Michael flew to Missouri at Christmastime, he had every intention of returning to Kabul in January to work with his leadership training organization and stay through the summer. In August, our friend, the international pastor in Kabul, had asked Michael to cover his position for five months. Adding a few months to our last year in Afghanistan had seemed fine—before my crisis with John had happened. Despite my early departure from ISK, Michael was determined to fulfill his promise to our friend.

But in January, some intense security events took place with Michael's company that stalled his return indefinitely. The early months of 2012 were tough on him, not knowing how to plan or what to give his attention to at home. I focused on my own renewal and re-entry, having no solutions for him, frustrated that he couldn't join me in a full-out effort to re-establish our lives in America.

His clearance to travel back to Afghanistan came in early April, but by then, we were only weeks away from the May 16th birth of granddaughter number two. The Kabul church had secured a substitute for the international pastor position who could stay till June 1st, so Michael arranged his departure for June 4th.

One April day, he shocked me with the question, "What if I asked you to come to Kabul with me?" He sat by me on the living room couch where I was reading. "I know you left with no intention of returning, but I feel I can do a better job in this pastor role with you beside me."

I put down my book. I was speechless, and frankly resistant to even considering his request.

Following the March debriefing seminar, I had started meeting weekly with three women from our support team. I had asked them to help me continue the self-review and assessment I had started, knowing I had to mine for the wisdom of the Afghanistan experience, each good and bad bit, to gain the full benefit.

These ladies and I discussed pertinent questions about how I responded to life's challenges and how I viewed myself through the eyes of God and others. These women were mature in their marriages, in their faith, in parenting skills, and in mentoring/teaching others, each one a leader in her own right. They were gracious, kind, funny, encouraging, yet honest to speak into my insecurities and self-doubt without false compliments or quick dismissals.

At the end of my next session with my supportive friends, I told them of Michael's Kabul-return request.

I started to cry. "What is the proper response when your husband asks you to do something, but you do not sense the same directive for yourself?"

They sat in empathetic silence for a few minutes. Their expressions said they did not wish me to re-enter Afghanistan any more than I did.

"Let's pray," one of them suggested. We held hands and bowed our heads. My tears continued throughout and I let my friends do the praying. After we finished, one of the women came over to me and knelt by my chair.

"Hold out for your own answer to this question, dear one. I think God will tell you what to do and you'll be confident one way or another." She hugged me tightly and lightly kissed my wet cheek.

I nodded and thanked her.

I hoped God would tell me, "*You are excused from this trip, Gail.*"

Two days after my group meeting, Michael was working on a sermon for the Sunday service at our home church. He had filled in for that pulpit regularly over the years. As would often transpire, he would research and think about his message for days but struggle keenly to hone the volume of information he'd amassed into a twenty- or thirty-minute speech.

I would hear outbursts like, "Why did I think I could be a preacher? I can't even make this sermon come together!" Or, "I don't know why anyone would listen to me. This is going to be terrible on Sunday!"

During these times, I would entice him into sanity by probing what he was trying to communicate, offer illustrations to help him show the practical application of his message, and generally draw him off the edge of anxiety. He would go back to his computer and, just in time for a couple of hours of sleep, finish his sermon.

And then he'd deliver it beautifully.

After performing my reality shake-down the Friday after my last meeting with my counselor-friends, he looked at me and said, "See, this is what I mean, hon. I need you to pop me out of my whirling during times like this. Please come to Kabul with me."

I looked away. "I don't know if I should. You know Sarah is asking to visit in early July with the girls while she is on maternity leave. She hasn't been able to come home in the summer for years. I want to help her with the new baby, give her time to rest, and play with Cora. Three-year-olds need lots of attention."

More than that, I had no desire to return to Kabul.

"Okay, I get that. I want that respite time for her, too. Come after that then." He patted my shoulder and gave me a hopeful look.

As I watched him go back to the study to polish off his sermon, I recognized the truth of what he spoke, how we make a powerful ministry team. And when he delivered his sermon

Sunday so expertly and with great impact on the congregation, I heard the call in my heart.

It will be okay for you to go with Michael to Kabul. I will go with you and your healing will not be interrupted. In fact, this will help. You'll see. Trust Me.

With a silent sob and teary vision as I sat in my pew, I saw a return to Afghanistan in my near future.

The Unveiled Truth: Being a counselor helped me know what to do after I was let go, but I couldn't do it alone. To move forward, I needed help from many sources along with solitude with God to get what I needed most from my reflections.

Trauma is real for most of us at some point in our lives. Avoiding or brushing it aside is not the proper response. Home can be a healing place. The familiarity and safety can help put some things on auto-pilot so we can focus on emotionally muscling toward new thoughts and behaviors.

Find ways to bring hurt and pain to light with people you trust. Write out feelings, read helpful books, cry, laugh, take breaks from reflecting, but then return to the *inside* work until you sense you have cleaned every closet and opened every door connected to the trauma.

Healing is possible. Press toward that end with all your heart, however broken it may be.

Have you asked someone you trust to help you debrief your pain and trauma?

20

Not Finished Yet

Sarah and my two sweet granddaughters left our Missouri home on July 10th after a fun ten-day visit. I'd wished our time would never end.

I left two days later for Afghanistan. My friends and family bit their tongues and shook their heads. The unspoken—or sometimes spoken—message was they did not think I was making a good decision by returning to the setting of my recent trauma, especially since the country's security was not improving. The news graphically reported recent repeated suicide and vehicle bombs exploding around Kabul.

The common parting comment I received from friends and family was, "Well, it might be a chance for you to get closure."

I then bit my tongue and shook my head. I felt no assurance this three-month visit would help me in any way. I was going only to accompany my husband. And because God said it would be *okay*.

Michael had been busy preparing the apartment for my arrival as well as adjusting to his new role in the expat community. I was glad to see him after our weeks apart, but honestly, I wasn't rejoicing to be back in Afghanistan.

Not being on the ISK campus for the first time in seven years was weird and required more housework of me than ever before. Without a cook or house cleaners, I had many tasks to keep me occupied, but then the lack of local language hit me hard. I could not shop or move around the city by myself easily because I could not communicate.

The summer heat was oppressive, and our upstairs apartment had lots of windows, making for an oven-like effect in the Kabul sunshine. There were few fans and no air conditioning. I wiped away sweat and battled self-pity.

In some ways, I felt like I'd returned to those early years in Kabul—missing my house, my family, my friends, and my convenient English-speaking life. Michael, however, seemed alive and elated.

He responded to my complaints with, "You could be happy if you chose to be."

Right. You're clearly content to be back in this hard place, but don't expect me to be happy. Not going to happen.

I could survive and rise out of my pity though, so I set my mind to doing so.

I exercised daily inside our spacious apartment bedroom and walked multiple boring laps on the concrete sidewalk along our Kabul compound yard in the coolness of the mornings. Outside the walls, Afghan construction workers poured concrete on high rise buildings and watched me walk. I wore a long, loose t-shirt and long yoga pants, but refused to wear a headscarf. I was inside my own property after all.

I wanted to scream, "Get over it! Stop staring and get back

to work!" I should have been used to it by then, but my seven-month hiatus had caused the maddening Afghan male habit of gawking to rile me again. It did make me walk faster in my frustration, so that was good.

Along with exercising my body, I chose to exercise my mind. I investigated the pastor's office library and read interesting books on leadership and cross-cultural memoirs.

Celeste still lived in Kabul, though she'd resigned from ISK along with many of the staff at the end of the year. Engaging with friends can do more for the soul than any amount of exercise and reading, so we got together often, which was such a bright spot in my summer. I also had social dates with former ISK students and their families. We visited Aqilla's family a couple of times and I shopped with her, always a rewarding experience with her knowledge of the language, culture, and great prices.

Michael wanted to encourage various international organization leaders living in Kabul through small gatherings and good food. To overcome my resistance to the increased workload in a place I struggled to purchase and prepare food properly for guests, he found an Afghan young man who cooked for us a couple of days each week. With the meal help, I found these group events delightful and stimulating.

Several times during that summer, I had invitations to assist Michael in personal or couples counseling. This was something we had done together in past years when Michael worked at churches in our hometown. While the physical and mental exercising was beneficial and a good use of my time, the opportunity to counsel captured my interest and lifted my spirit much more.

We met with a Dutch man dealing with panic attacks, so I helped him work through desensitization steps to manage his responses. He sent us a note of thanks and some wonderful coffee in gratitude.

A couple wanting pre-engagement counseling came to us. She was a practical, kind Midwestern woman, and he was a smiling, romantic Indian man. They met working in Kabul and fell in love early in their relationship. Both knew there were important issues to focus on before marriage. Counseling people from other cultures proved challenging and interesting. I looked forward to each session. They eventually married and now have two children, still working with Afghans through video media, his specialty.

A former ISK mother, who had worked part-time at the school before and after I left, came to see us. She poured out her hurt and anger due to the difficulties she'd encountered with the school administration, mainly John.

"It was so hurtful, and I am struggling to forgive. I know I need to let this go and trust God, but I am not making much progress." She wept in these confessions and I joined her. The stories she shared mirrored some of my own.

I had much understanding and empathy for her situation, so I shared methods of my personal journey of healing with her. As I advised, she diligently journaled and reflected on what lessons she needed to learn from her experience. We worked hard to guard our conversation from turning into a gripe fest, stay positive, and find the strength to forgive and release the offenses, mostly caused by the same people.

A catastrophic event happened during our summer stint in Kabul. An American, Al Geiser, and his Afghan business partner were shot on July 23rd while traveling from a worksite in Bamiyan back to Kabul. Who committed the murder or why was often speculated upon but remained unconfirmed despite the FBI investigation.

Michael had to make full arrangements for the body and burial, as well as care for the widow and grieving friends and extended family. I joined him in visits with fellow expats, debriefing the crisis and offering support as best I could.

Walking through the British cemetery after Al's funeral, seeing the numerous headstones of former friends and aid workers who were murdered or died while serving Afghans was a somber, and yet inspiring moment.

We all die. The key is to make your life count. Giving your life for something or someone significant is not a waste, it is a life well-lived. So, what is next for me to commit to whole-heartedly?

The opportunities I'd been having to use my counseling skills yielded such positive, grateful responses from the clients and friends that I felt God was saying: *Here is what you can do when you return home, counsel people again.*

I recalled my joy in helping people sort through past traumas and work toward a more satisfying future before coming to ISK. The counseling I was doing that summer, not only helped others, but was helping me. For the first time since I'd left ISK, I had some sense of direction.

As always, in August, the ISK team would arrive in Kabul. With the campus being only ten minutes away from our church, I wondered how I would react when the staff came to a service for the first time. Most of the faces would be new after the mass exodus of teachers in June, but there would be a few left to whom I had said a teary goodbye eight months ago. John was no longer the director, so I had no worries about an encounter with him.

As teachers stepped out of the school vehicles and others arrived on foot that first Friday service, I was hugged and greeted warmly. I introduced myself to many new team members and truly enjoyed the time. Besides friendly smiles, many of the veteran ISK staff had tears in their eyes when we embraced. Later, I pondered in prayer what had caused their emotional display, when I felt only happiness at our reunion.

I then realized I had spent the past months intentionally analyzing my grief and trauma, working toward a fresh outlook, and generally resting and healing. I had been successful at moving on. However, my former team members, upon seeing me again, were basically thrust right back into the pain of last fall.

I decided—and my hospitality-driven husband agreed—to invite small groups of ISK staff to hang out at our apartment, so these dear folks could begin to release their concern for me once they recognized I had grown from last fall's trauma and was getting on with life. We watched funny movies, popped popcorn, played games, and caught up with each other's personal lives and families.

Once school started, the new ISK director asked Celeste and me to consider subbing on the ISK campus. We were both shocked by the invitation, thinking our presence would not be welcome. The numerous vacated positions had not been fully filled when school started, so we guessed the new administration felt rather desperate.

After a couple of days of prayer and serious thought, I decided to decline. I didn't want to look like I quit caring about the success of ISK, but I did not want to answer questions from students and families about my leaving or possible return either. Information from the past administration had been sparse about my departure, and I determined I would not take on the responsibility of trying to make sense of their actions. Returning to campus on a day-to-day basis might also undo my recent and ongoing healing.

Then an idea of how to help without hurting myself came to me after receiving a couple of phone calls.

"Gail, I have no idea what I'm doing. This was basically dropped in my lap and I could use some help, if you don't mind." The new, untrained ISK school counselor was tasked with admitting new students and working through transcripts and credits for high school students.

Perfect! Here is a way to help my beloved ISK without putting myself at too much emotional risk. Thank you, God!

I invited the counselor to bring her pile of paperwork over anytime she needed. Her top-quality administrative skills and past year's experience in the ISK front office served her well. She quickly had the job well in hand and went on to complete a school counseling degree, continuing in international schools with her science teacher husband when they left ISK.

Next door to our compound lived a couple from the Netherlands, who became a delightful part of our summer experience. They were career overseas workers, first in Bangladesh and now Afghanistan. The husband had hosted the monthly leader prayer gatherings I had appreciated in years past. As neighbors, we shared meals together, stories about our grown children, and the state of international aid in the country. They had a wonderful realistic, yet also optimistic, view of things.

The wife and I met several times for coffee and prayer. I gleaned much refreshment from our times together. Her review of my recent experiences left me feeling affirmed and hopeful for the future. Her training as a psychiatric nurse surely came in handy for mentoring me as I continued my healing process.

One night, the couple popped over to chat. Not long into

the conversation, the husband mentioned an important position in his organization that had become available.

"Gail, I think you would do well in this job. The decisiveness you employed when managing a large staff like you did at ISK would serve you well. This would give you a reason to stay in Kabul with Michael." He listed as many details as he could about the selection process and the international scope of the NGO where he served as the Executive Director.

I was very flattered and surprised. Michael's eyes lit up with hope.

"My being a woman would not be an issue in such a top-level position?" I asked our friend, although I knew as a predominately European organization, gender equality was well-respected.

"Not at all." He took another sip of his tea and smiled enthusiastically at me. His wife also nodded in agreement.

I was complimented by his offer and tempted—not because it gave me the opportunity to live in Afghanistan again, but because I'd get to work under our neighbor's administration. I admired this couple so much and I knew I could learn a great deal about leadership and global organizations from him as my boss.

"So, can we talk about this?" Michael waited until the couple went home to turn toward me. "You heard what he said, and I agree you would be great in that role. What do you think?"

I knew he was hoping beyond hope for me to consider coming back to Afghanistan. "I need to think and pray. This is big and I had no preparation for what he offered tonight." Looking straight at my husband, I stated, "Don't press me, Michael, please. I know what you want, and I'll take that into consideration, but I have to figure this out for me and for our family, too." I turned away and began to gather our teacups on a tray.

After a couple of days of serious reflection and hot, sleepless nights, I knew I could not take the job. Besides having to remain in Afghanistan and be apart from our kids and grandkids again, we would need to raise our own salaries which many global workers did, but I did not want that kind of financial stress. An even bigger influence was that our friend was preparing to retire from his executive position soon.

My newfound wisdom from the last few years rang in my head: *There are two parts to every job, the job itself and who you work for*. I was not willing to risk the chance that the next boss in this organization would be a train wreck for me in the difficult environment of a third-world country.

Been there, done that, and had the scars to show for it.

Still, the job opportunity bolstered my wobbly self-confidence and gave me even more assurance that God was not yet done with me. Michael was disappointed but accepted my decision. I am sure he wanted to talk much more about it, but wisely kept his comments to a minimum.

One of my favorite times from that summer involved Khalid and a family with three teenage sons. Khalid was in Kabul to help ISK with some lease agreements. The father of the teen boys had met Khalid many years back as a young adult and had helped him learn English and invited him into their home often. The mother of this family came from Scotland and her husband from Ireland, but the family came to Afghanistan by way of New Zealand.

Two of the boys had attended ISK during my time as principal. The whole family exuded cheerful, positive attitudes combined with resourcefulness and realism. The couple worked hard in NGO activities and had a rich global view of their place in the world, helping others and embracing cultural differences.

I called the family and Khalid with an invitation to join us at the apartment. "Come for dinner. We'd love to catch up."

With six men to feed, I asked Michael to go to a local shop and find a beef roast. He purchased a top quality, five-pound roast from a trusted storekeeper's freezer. I planned to add mashed potatoes and the trimmings to delight my guests with un-Afghan fare. Though I was no stranger to cooking for a group, I still worried a bit about the unfamiliar utensils and appliances.

However, I had not expected unfamiliar *meat*. When the frosted packaging cleared during thawing the day before our dinner, I read with shock: *water buffalo tenderloin*.

What? I had no idea how to cook water buffalo!

The internet is a great gift in so many ways. I searched and read about the need to roast water buffalo with plenty of moisture to keep the low-fat meat from drying out. I found a soy sauce recipe for basting the roast while in the oven. Michael and I decided to say nothing about our special dish until after the meal and see if anyone commented. We knew the family to be great pranksters with robust senses of humor and felt no concern about offending them.

Michael sliced the cooked tenderloin in thick pieces. I piled up the massive amount of mashed potatoes in bowls and filled the bread baskets with French bread from our friends' nearby bakery. Green beans, carrots, and lots of gravy rounded out the menu.

My Scottish friend took a deep sniff when she entered the kitchen and remarked, "Oh, yes, roast beef and taters! Whenever we go home, all my family and friends try to please me with my favorite comfort foods! How did you know?" She hugged me appreciatively and rubbed her hands together in delight.

I smiled at her and said, "Just a lucky guess! Everything is ready so let's eat while the food is hot." Michael grinned at me as we ushered all six hungry guests to seats and set the food before them.

We enjoyed boisterous conversation with such lively personalities present. The teenage boys made short work of their first platefuls and requested seconds of everything. Soon the platters and serving bowls were empty, and compliments had been offered.

Michael cleared his throat for attention and asked, "Anyone notice anything different about our meat tonight?"

Quizzical looks passed around the table. One of the boys said, "What was it—not cow?"

"No, any guesses?" Michael was enjoying the riddle time. The alert eyes and widening grins signaled interest but no one had a guess.

When we revealed they'd eaten water buffalo, Khalid clapped in appreciation for the surprise. The fun-loving boys were intrigued, but not aghast. "Really? All right! We've had camel tongue, kangaroo sausages, and snails, but this is our first water buffalo." We all laughed and went on to homemade pie and ice cream for dessert.

More than I, Michael was sad to leave at the end of September when our friends returned to resume their positions at the international church. But as much as he wanted to stay, Michael recognized that our time in Afghanistan had finally come to an end. We had enjoyed visiting with so many wonderful people over the years. Our final week there, we said our last goodbyes to as many Afghan and international friends as possible, without so much heartache as there'd been in December 2011.

All in all, those three summer months went well, and I did not regret returning. The opportunity to impact others in a ministry-related role helped me to discover what the next chapter of my life could look like. I was glad Michael, and God, had convinced me to go.

The Unveiled Truth: Everyone has value and a contribution to make. After returning to Kabul that summer, I began to believe in future service for myself—that God wasn't done with my life.

Negative experiences can be a setback in confidence and inspiration, but we can look to past positives amidst the trials. We can discover anew what skills and talents we possess that impact others for good. Not everyone is going to approve or applaud us, but there will be those who do.

Seek inspiration from past successes for the direction of your life. Let difficulties weave into the tapestry of your story but not define or defeat you.

God isn't finished with me—or you—until our last breath.

What failures are you letting define you instead of successes? What steps can you list to help you move past them and focus on the positive?

21

Learning and Living Well

While working on the first draft of this book, I received news that ISK might be closing before the end of the 2014-2015 school year.

Rumors began flying during the winter break, and I received Facebook messages and emails asking me if I knew what was going on. Of course I had no inside information, being now a full-fledged outsider with few friends left on campus from my years as principal.

On February 1, 2015, ISK closed. For good.

The official Oasis administrative statement about shutting down ISK read: *The elevated threat against the school, staff, and students caused us to make the most difficult of calls.*

Soon I began to read angry postings on social media by students and alumni accusing the school personnel of being cowards and using security as an excuse for financial problems or Western selfishness. After studying in English for years, most Afghan ISK students could not return to local schools easily with their minimal local language skills. They felt abandoned and used that word frequently in their rants.

ISK had become less safe during my time in Kabul, and the situation had continually grown worse since my departure. Daily bombings and attacks occurred throughout the city and countryside. During 2014, several key security incidents impacted the international community as well as ISK.

On March 28, 2014, Taliban assailants attacked the very compound where Michael and I had been living during our 2012 summer assignment in Kabul. Around thirty expats hid in an upstairs bathroom for hours listening to gunfire. They were later rescued unharmed. Civilian foreigners were becoming direct targets more often.

Less than a month after the Taliban attack on the community center, three men were fatally shot at CURE International hospital, including Dr. Jerry Umanos, a popular pediatrician whose wife worked for me at ISK. International organizations began to pull out more families with women and children to reduce risks.

One of the most painful occurrences happened on November 29th, 2014 to a South African family who had been in Afghanistan for twelve years. Werner Groenewald and his two teenage children who had attended ISK during my time were killed at their home by three Taliban trespassers with machine guns and grenades. Their physician mother, Hannelie, was away from home. She was spared the terror of the shootings, but not the pain of losing her family.

In earlier terrorist activity in Afghanistan, the targets were mostly government and military personnel and men, not women and children, and not schools. The killing of the innocent Groenewald children struck anger and deep fear in the hearts of international families and even Afghan parents. A school and cultural center built by the French government for the local people that was often used for plays and concert performances by ISK was then attacked in early December.

A wind of hopelessness blew through every corner of Afghan society, even prompting the resignation of the Kabul Chief of Police, General Zahir Zahir. No one, Afghan or expat, felt safe anymore or seemed to know how to improve the situation.

What was ISK to do to keep its students and staff out of harm's way?

I am sure the administration did what I did back in my principal years, contacting the government-employed parents and U.S. advisors to get counsel. If ISK was advised to close, what else could be done? Who would want to take responsibility for a child, teacher, or Afghan worker not leaving school one day due to an attack?

I checked Facebook postings and emails like an addict several times a day in February and March 2015. I wanted to read every related news article and comment. Most students and staff expressed appreciation for the almost ten years of ISK and all that was done to offer quality education to Afghans in a desperate situation.

As the word of the school's closing circulated among my own friends and family, I received sympathy and encouragement to believe that what I had invested in the school was not wasted. I held fast to the truth of these statements. One day, I decided to write my own thoughts and feelings about the situation on a private ISK Facebook page. I hoped to counteract the pervasive discouragement of the students and families left without ISK and offer my own wounded-but-now-healed perspective about forced change.

While I typed out my thoughts, tears flowed unchecked. I had to edit out some of my more radical comments aimed at the complainers who denounced ISK staff with labels of weakness or selfishness. Those judgments were unfair, but would the accusers listen? Probably not, and I was not interested in a Facebook debate, which some ISK alumni students had tried to undertake against these negative voices but hadn't seemed successful. I wrote:

> One of the beautiful things about education is, even when you can't immediately see the fruit yielded, you don't have to doubt its value on a daily basis if done with dedication and sincerity of heart. I have personally wondered how other jobs could begin to compare with a teacher's impact. ISK exemplifies this mystery.
>
> When we started the school in 2005, there was a hope and vision for investing in future global leaders through the hard work of foreign professional educators and the sacrifice of loving families in a war-torn place without much future stability. We went literally day-to-day for many years at various turbulent times. But we knew the seeds could grow in these young, precious minds, so we sowed with all our might for the time we were given.
>
> In our almost ten years as ISK, God has granted that we saw a glimpse of the fruit of our labors, and it is excellent and encouraging. Breaking barriers of tribal prejudices in Afghanistan and learning to work through cross-cultural differences happened every day across the ISK campus from preschool to high school. These are the leaders of tomorrow, not just for hurting Afghanistan, but also for a troubled world who needs what these young men and women have learned.

> The time for ISK seed-sowing has been stopped, but the fruit will continue to grow and ripen. We will be looking for you, ISK students, in your places around the globe. Make us proud, for yourself, your family, your country, and for ISK.
>
> Much love, Mr. & Mrs. Goolsby

Many former students responded with kindness and gratitude to my message. Some still wondered if attending ISK without graduating was worth the now challenging transition to continue education somewhere else.

Was it worth seven years of my life to live and work in Afghanistan now that ISK was no more?

Absolutely.

The closing of ISK did nothing to change the value of the time I spent in Kabul. My list of gains may fall short of the list of sacrifices in pure number, but the sacrifices have faded in significance whereas the gains have become woven into the fabric of my being, my thoughts, attitudes, and actions. I am different, in positive ways.

I may have originally felt caught in God's net and moved to Afghanistan without much excitement or appreciation for the rare opportunity, but I benefitted through the difficulties. I know things about the world and myself now that likely never would have surfaced without going through the trials I experienced in Afghanistan.

Like many who leave their homeland for lesser-developed places, I came to regard things like sidewalks, driving myself, electricity, central heat, schools, libraries, and hamburgers as wonderful things, no longer an American birthright. The multiple freedoms and conveniences I enjoy as an American, an American woman, now mean a great deal more to me, and I recognized fully what our military personnel do around the world to protect and provide such gifts.

Each time over the seven years I traveled back home from ISK, when the U.S. customs agent returned my stamped passport and said, "Welcome home," I only nodded my thanks, unable to respond due to the lump in my throat. Every single time. My country is far from perfect, but I am not ashamed to identify myself as an American and a Christ-follower, and in all my worldly travels, I try harder than ever to represent the best of our nation and my faith.

After such exposure and engagement with diverse people and cultures, I am committed to become acquainted beyond first impressions or stereotypes of those I encounter. I purpose to spend time interacting with the Jordanian hairstylist at my salon, the Iranian sisters at my workplace, the Congolese families at my church, and the Afghan families and international students in my town. Each year, I save needed funds for global travel where under-resourced people need help. I try to share my education and counseling skills as best I can in difficult situations.

I have a newfound patience and flexibility for the unplanned, uncontrolled events of life after so many challenges during the Kabul years. Often I hear *oh, well* in my mind as I make adjustments for interruptions or changes in schedules. Just doesn't seem so important or realistic anymore to expect things to always be the way I want them. Rather, un-American, isn't it?

In my journey to expand my self-awareness after my Kabul departure, I found new acknowledgment of my personal ability to influence, accomplish, and pioneer worthwhile projects. These insights included increased confidence in the power of teamwork and a deeper understanding of the truth that there is more than one way to do things right. I believe I now possess the strength to face physical danger and daily frustrations better than ever before.

My family did not suffer irreparable damage in my choice to leave the U.S. While I never wanted to leave my precious children to go overseas, I gained tremendous pride in their ability to navigate adulthood—without my help. They were amazing decision-makers and disciplined students (for the most part) during our absence, and I see the maturity muscles they were forced to develop (perhaps too soon in their opinions) serving them well today. I was able to be present for both granddaughters' births during this timeframe and be with my father during school breaks and for his last week on earth.

As for Michael, the person I blame for taking me to Kabul not once but twice, we experienced so much together, our marriage is much richer and bound tighter. Few would understand our shared memories and stories. But we get it, and even with our cumulative scars, we are thankful we went to Afghanistan—together. In the times that really counted, we were each other's champion, not just an irritant. I always knew he wanted the best for me as I did for him. I wouldn't have grown to the depths and lengths I enjoy today if he hadn't proposed the Afghanistan adventure on that Caribbean cruise years ago.

People often remark how brave I was to move to Afghanistan, to serve as a woman leader in a male-dominated culture, to leave my home and children behind, and to work so hard in a desperate, will-it-really-matter place to help students learn and achieve their dreams to graduate and go to college. I know that although I had to be snatched up by a "net" to get me there, it was not really brave. It was right, it was glorious, and I am left forever changed.

All of us should learn to live well the life we have been given.

And you are just as capable as I am, to go out, and better the world. When an opportunity comes along to help humankind, no matter how scary or crazy or dreadful you might think it is, take the time to consider if it might be your own Afghanistan—a hard time of trial that reaps you more rewards than you could possibly dream—and if it is, commit to it wholeheartedly, trusting that God will be beside you, helping you improve the world, by most importantly, helping you become a better you.

Anna, John, Michael, and Gail in Kabul, August 2005.

Evidence of decades of war and damage could be seen on buildings in Kabul and all over Afghanistan.

Returning refugees poured into Kabul with inadequate water, electricity, roads, and jobs. They built mud houses up the surrounding mountainsides.

Khalid and Byron at the first parent meeting of ISK in September 2005. (This was held on the back porch of the admin building.)

Gail at Wardak village girls' school in the fall of 2005.

Wardak village boys taking an exam with their teacher. (He's holding a wooden "sword" to discourage cheating and maintain order.)

Kabul schoolgirls utilizing umbrellas to shade themselves from the high desert sun as they walk to afternoon classes.

U.S. Lt. General William Caldwell, commander of NATO Training Mission-Afghanistan, reads to elementary students in the ISK library.

Majestic mountains in northern Afghanistan before the snowfall.

October snow on mountains surrounding Kabul seen from the ISK campus.

Our beloved ISK staff chef, Sakhi.

"Mr. Mike" with some ISK national staff, including Ali second from right.

ISK school buildings and connecting courtyards.

High school music and choir concert with tents, chairs, carpets, and toshaks behind the ISK buildings utilizing back porches for the stage.

ISK staff 2009-2010...front row: Gail next to Karen...Celeste at the end.

Gail conferring U.S. high school diplomas for the ISK Class of 2009 at the InterContinental Hotel Ballroom in Kabul.

Gail at a press conference with Minister of Education Hanif Atmar October 2008 as ISK is officially recognized as a registered international school in Afghanistan.

Mrs. Laura Bush visits with ISK students (left) and Khalid (right of Mrs. Bush) at the U.S. Embassy in June 2008.

PACE-A training at ISK with Aqilla (left) translating literacy materials to the Afghan Ministry of Education leaders.

ISK choir performs at U.S. Embassy in Kabul.

Gail and Mary at Lake Quargha outside of Kabul.

ISK driver, guard, and the armored car used to take Gail and a friend, visiting from the U.S., to a nearby village.

Presidential Palace luncheon with ISK government class, John, Gail, and teachers as guests of Chief of Staff Daudzai.

President Hamid Karzai greets ISK government students and staff in perfect English.

Michael and Gail with Aqilla, her daughter, daughter-in-law, and sister-in-law.

Charlene, Michael, and Gail on the Great Wall during China trip November 2011.

Gail's last ISK housing assignment with Charlene across from the admin building. This is the back yard garden view with the rose bushes.

Fall 2011 farewell recognition luncheon at Palace hosted by ISK fathers, Minister of Education, and Mayor of Kabul.

Acknowledgments

"You should write your stories down. People need to hear about the truths of Afghanistan and its people, not just what is on the news."

I heard this type of comment often during my years at ISK and upon returning home. In the same way, I'd never planned to go to Afghanistan, I never dreamed of writing a book. Many people had a part in what I learned those seven years in Kabul and bringing this project to its completion and I am extremely grateful.

Janeen – Your own writing experience and skills gave me a place to start. You listened to my goals and are the only person I let read the original drafts as I pulled the stories from my mind to the page. Thanks for the companionship when I began this now five-year adventure.

Deb – How would I have known our beginnings in coaching six years ago would turn into a tight bond over writing as well as sharing life? My confidence has grown as you honestly reviewed my steps in joining the writing industry and gave me your realistic, yet optimistic counsel.

Kathy – When I had no answer to your question at the 2015 Tulsa conference about my writing niche, you gently probed me to identify myself as an author. Your remark, which exactly answered my prayer request to God, "I think we can find the next step for your manuscript," made me cry then and still smile broadly today. Your coaching, personal concern, and WordGirls experiences set me on a good path for entering the world of writing.

Donna K., Elaine, John W., Sarah K., and Dilip – I appreciated your encouragement as those further down the book publishing path. Our brief conversations were like a drink of cool water when my dry throat needed refreshment to continue.

Celeste – *For such a time as this* describes our God-given friendship as we walked together during the Kabul years as women administrators, striving to bring ISK to the best level of education possible in war-torn Afghanistan. More than that, you offered loyalty and understanding in my darkest time. Even now, separated Kansas to California, one phone call puts us together and finds us still sharing life lessons.

Karen, Ken, Khalid, Katie, Charlene, and other ISK team members – The stories in this book do not give full credit for the role you played in forming me as a school leader and mature Christian. All of you inspire me with your giftings and obedience to follow God, even when it is hard, very hard. You left a powerful impact on ISK and the students there. Well done.

Aqilla, Sakhi, Habib, Nurallah, Ali, Asef, Reza, and the Salimee, Daudzai, Khalq, Mehdi families – You pulled back the veil on Afghan hospitality and loyalty, inviting me into your home and showing care, kindness, and appreciation for my time at ISK. There would not have been an ISK without people like you believing in our vision.

Byron – I hope I did you proud in capturing bits of our time in Kabul. We may have raised the roof at times in our working together, but we made a solid leadership team, and ISK was a fine school. If you hadn't had that inconvenient 2008 heart attack, well, this would have been a very different story, wouldn't it?! 😊

Tim, Patti, Jim, Bernice, Pat, Joan, Susan R., Donna A., Dave, Donna, Nel, Dirk, Ken E., Debbie E., Steve, Kathi, Tiia, Pat, Graham, and other expat friends – You all made the Kabul time bearable, richer, and even fun with non-ISK activities and finding God at work in and around us.

Joe, Steve, Susan L., and Oasis staff – There would not have been an ISK without your vision and investment back in 2003 with Kabul International Academy. I never doubted your commitment to quality education and using this platform to transform young minds and hearts for the glory of God and the good of the world. Keep going.

Mary and the SMAG team – Mary, there would not have been a call to Kabul without you leading teams to Pakistan and Afghanistan in the 2000s and your personal passion. You and the SMAG team served and loved us and our precious kids, along with helping us re-enter with your continuing friendship. No cross-cultural worker ever had a better sending team than the Goolsbys and we will cherish each one of you, forever.

Brookdale Church Family – From our first couple of years as a young married couple in 1979 to our return in 2001, you always loved us and offered us a home at Brookdale. You gave us a place to process our time in Kabul each visit home and supported us financially as well as relationally for many years. Saying goodbye in 2015 was hard, but our memories remain wonderfully sweet.

Charlotte, Melody, Ellen, Jeff, Debbie, Cindy, Kat, Rich, Connie, Danny, and St. Joseph Christian School staff and families – My confidence and foundation to take on the principal role at ISK was built on years of learning how to best reach the hearts and minds of students for eternity with you.

Lydia – My role model for *grace under fire* and *excellence is possible if you work hard enough.* Everything I learned about caring for teachers and creating a team atmosphere came from my years under your leadership. We have traveled many roads together, dear friend, some full of Missouri potholes and Kabul landmines, but having company during the journey made all the difference.

My Wisdom/Prayer Team: Heidi, Janiece, Teresa, Salli, Pam, Diana, Ailene, Judy, Roberta, Sandra, Deborah – For the past four years you let me celebrate and complain about the long, seemingly endless journey for this book and my little life, rebooting everything in our move to Wichita in 2015. You represent some of the best aspects of my past, present, and no doubt future as I continue to *Learn to Live Well.* Bless each of you wonderful women!

Melissa – God was incredibly good and kind to bring our paths together in windy Wichita. Your professional editing and storytelling skills brought my Kabul tales to a new light and took the value for the reader to a new level. What started out fuzzy and discouraging in rewriting the complete manuscript, ended up satisfying to me and hopefully worthwhile for us both. So grateful for all your expertise and direction to bringing this project to completion.

Tony – How generous you were to offer your design skills for this project. May God richly bless you in return for assisting God's people in their desire to create with excellence.

Sarah, Anna, and John (Jason and Jordan, too) – What amazing adults you are! I couldn't be prouder of how you navigated the Kabul years on your own. Thanks for not closing off your heart and mind to the crazy idea of your parents moving to Afghanistan and even risking a visit. Your own hearts for reaching the world in your individual spheres of influence is impressive and reveals a love for God as you love His people. Your many gifts and talents are being well used, and your dad and I are so delighted in watching you learn your lessons well and make your life count.

Michael – It was all your fault, my love, that this story even happened. I hope it was what you envisioned when you presented the idea on that cruise ship sixteen years ago, but really, how could we have known what was before us? We did it—together—the best way we knew how, with lots of people assisting. The challenges caused our relationship to stretch, ache, and grow into something even more reliable and wonderful. I love you with all my heart.

My God – I felt your presence in the best and worst of my times in Kabul. You led me there, taught me new truths, sustained me, and brought me home. I shared how personal you are to me with those who see you only as a distant Creator and afterlife Judge. I now understand more about your hopes and plans for this world you made and the diverse people groups who live here. I hope I served you well in Kabul.

About the Author

Gail Goolsby has spent her entire career in some form of education—classroom, school counselor, principal, personal counseling, life coaching, parenting, and now even grandparenting. She has taught all ages and especially enjoys kindergartners who love their teacher every day and find that all learning is new and exciting.

Gail grew up in Virginia. While interning in Washington, DC with a youth leadership organization, she met her husband, Michael. She then moved to the Mid-West, graduating from Oklahoma State University with a degree in Family Relations/Child Development and a license to teach grades K-8. She holds an MA in Professional Counseling from Liberty University and MEd in Educational Leadership from Regent University.

After returning from Afghanistan, Gail pursued coaching training with Creative Results Management (Keith Webb) and achieved her ACC credential from the International Coach Federation. She started her *Learn to Live Well* business in 2013 and continues counseling, coaching, speaking, writing, and teaching either face-to-face or virtually around the world.

Gail has three grown children, two sons-in-law, and three granddaughters. She makes her home with her pastor husband of forty-one years in Wichita, KS where the wind comes sweeping down the plain and proves there really is no place like home.

Find her at www.gailgoolsby.com

CPSIA information can be obtained
at www.ICGtesting.com
Printed in the USA
LVHW041926040422
715267LV00003B/361

9 781734 243611